THE ARCHITECTURE OF
BUILDING SERVICES

THE ARCHITECTURE OF BUILDING SERVICES

GORDON NELSON

B. T. BATSFORD LTD · LONDON

© Gordon Nelson
First published 1995

Typeset by Servis Filmsetting Ltd, Manchester

and printed in Great Britain by The Bath Press, Avon

for the publishers
B.T. Batsford Ltd
4 Fitzhardinge Street
London W1H 0AH

A CIP catalogue record for this book is available from
the British Library.

ISBN 0 7134 7381 9

CONTENTS

ACKNOWLEDGEMENTS

This book is dedicated to the several hundred students who made it necessary, and, for their patient encouragement, to Professors Mike Martin of California and Derek Poole of Cardiff.

My thanks are due to many who have helped and encouraged me. The following have given direct help or provided information and illustrations: Building Services Research and Information Association; Chartered Institute of Building Services Engineers; Arup Associates, Architects + Engineers + Quantity Surveyors; Ahrends Burton & Koralek, Architects; Sir Norman Foster and Partners, Architects; Oxford Architects Partnership; Renton Howard Wood Levin Partnership; J. Roger Preston and Partners, Consulting Engineers; Whitby and Bird, Consulting Engineers; Dr David Lord, California Polytechnic State University; Professor Derek Poole; Dr Hugh Byrd; Ami-Rad Limited; Carrier Air Conditioning; Hoval Limited; ABB Flakt Products.

PREFACE

INTRODUCTION

There are available many excellent books that describe both the physical and operating characteristics of heating, ventilating and air-conditioning systems; however, few, if any, address the integration of such systems in the building design process. This book attempts to redress the balance by explaining environmental control systems through the eyes of the designers of buildings, rather then provide yet another text book for the specialist engineer.

Ensuring that acceptable environmental conditions are maintained in a public building, throughout the shifts and changes in the external climate, demands at least one type of environmental control system – no matter how simple it may be. Space will always be required within the building in which to accommodate some part of such a system; even the humble open fire needs a chimney planned for it. The amount of space needed and the complexity of its disposition will quite obviously be a function of the type of system needed, a hospital or laboratory will call for a far more technical installation than say a primary school. It is ironic therefore that, given such an obvious statement, its implications are so often ignored by the designers of buildings. The allocation of space in a building is in too many instances a retrospective and palliative design activity, and one that seldom plays a part at the strategic stage of design. Given such a situation it is hardly surprising that the proper provision of space is the exception rather than the rule and that substantial changes to a design are often required.

This situation arises for several reasons. Chief amongst these is the importance that some architectural tutors attach to design activities other than the more technical subjects and that the projects they set for their students tend to reflect that bias. It is natural that designers, who define architecture as being more an art than a science, will concentrate more on the aesthetic form of the building and its

place in the stylistic idiom of the moment. The so-called technologies, which give a habitable form to the design and include such items as pipes and ducts, will come low down on their list of priorities when they are absorbed by 'the design' – whatever that may mean.

However, a desire to follow the style of a design hero need not necessarily lead to the neglect of those technologies; indeed it can promote them to a high priority. There is ample precedent to support this argument, some of it of recent years and even more of it from past masters. Examples from the work of Lloyd Wright and Louis Kahn are discussed in the book; it was the latter who coined the phrase 'servant and served spaces' and instead of neglecting the allocation of space for systems made it part of the architectural statement.

In order to ensure that proper space is allocated it is necessary to know something about what it is that needs the space and what 'it' does. The selection of a suitable environmental control system, or at least the 'hardware' part of it, is generally a logical process – identify the problem and seek a solution. But the hardware is only one part of the system, the other part is the building – and the design process of that is rarely a logical process. We will look at both processes as we go through the book.

You could of course consider the building services as a bolt-on solution. If you truly believe that then put the book back on the shelf and expect the complaint that is so often heard: 'the architect made a mess of it and now we have to put a system in that will make the building livable.'

I have used the term 'environmental control system' with care, particularly the word 'system'. If our buildings are to be a delight to be in, then what I have called the 'hardware' and the building that you provide must work together, if not an example of symbiotic harmony then at least an example of synergy.

HOW TO USE THE BOOK

You can if you wish read it from cover to cover, but I would be just as happy if you dipped in to find what you want and got it. It is not laid out like the usual text book about systems, in that it does not always progress in a logical and orderly fashion. Chapter One, for example, explores some ideas about design methods and then focuses on some starting points that are particularly apt as far as this book is concerned. Chapter Two takes that chosen focus and reviews some useful rules of thumb that may be applied in conjunction with it to produce a certain type of building; it also presents an overview of what needs to be understood about the basis of those rules so that their limitations are realized.

Chapter Three develops the idea of design strategies and looks at planning the internal space of a building and how this relates to the choice of environmental control systems.

Chapter Four, before describing systems, examines the possible reasons for their application, then proceeds to describe how heat may be generated and the means of its transportation through a distribution system. Horizontal and vertical distributory methods are explained together with the relationship of the shape and disposition of services cores and certain types of buildings.

Chapter Five marks the beginning of the examination of the various types of environmental control systems, starting with the simple heating system and its components and covering the operating characteristics that are significant in their selection.

Chapter Six continues the focus on systems and describes how warm-air systems operate and how their various components contribute to the performance and physical characteristics.

Chapter Seven features the full air-conditioning system. It starts with an overview of the study of psychrometrics (the science of the behaviour of a mass of moist air), explains the various conditioning processes and concludes by describing the components of air-conditioning systems.

Chapter Eight brings the more formal text to a close by describing the means of introducing air into a room. It explains why a mass of air follows certain predictable patterns of movement within a room and how the knowledge of this may influence the choice of terminal outlets.

Chapters Nine and Ten are both Design Exercises. These demonstrate how the book, and other sources of information, may be used to first select a suitable environmental control system and later determine how much space is needed for the accommodation of its components.

Chapters Eleven through to Fifteeen are Case Studies of buildings that are exemplars of their type, and demonstrates how well-known architects and engineers have designed environmental control systems for the buildings.

Associated with the text you will find appropriate space allocation diagrams. These will help you to determine how much space is needed for the systems. They are also repeated in the Appendix together with a version of a type of a flow chart. The intention is to help you to quickly pick out information you will need about the choice of systems and the space they need during the design process. For ease of assembly it is presented as a sequential process, but by now you should know that the action of designing is rarely that convenient. Use it if it helps in whole or in part.

Each chapter has references to text books, papers resulting from research and articles from various journals. You should follow these up because they provide not only information that will be relevant to your project work but also discuss in greater depth many of the subjects only touched upon in this text. For additional information see Further Reading on page 156.

CHAPTER ONE

DESIGN METHODS

METHODOLOGY

Designing: *The performing of a very complicated act of faith.* (Jones, 1966)

'Where shall I begin your Majesty?' he asked. 'Begin at the beginning,' the King said, gravely, 'and go on till you come to the end; then stop.'

Obviously the King, the one in Lewis Carroll's *Alice's Adventures in Wonderland*, had never designed anything. In reality it is more likely to be 'Start at what you think is the beginning, and go on until the end; or what you think is the end'.

Starting any project is a challenge for most of us, whether we are writers or the designers of buildings; staring at that blank sheet of paper can be daunting. If you are not too sure what to do first with a design project, then take comfort that you are not alone and, as you will see shortly, there are techniques that will get you started.

Although this book is not strictly about design methods it too must start somewhere, so let us commence by looking, albeit briefly, at the ways in which some designers order their thought processes. Many seasoned architects will tell you that they do not have a method, their approach is said to be 'intuitive'. However, some decisions that are said to have been made intuitively are in truth based upon forgotten knowledge. In the 1950s and '60s design methodology featured on the syllabus of many schools of architecture; however, it was seen to be aligned with functionalism and to a large extent lost favour as the modern movement was

found to be flawed. It is possible, therefore, that today's tutors, who absorbed the methods when they were students have forgotten the fact and now regard their approach as being an intuitive process.

One way to start is with a notion of a design, or better still a concept, which as it develops will integrate things that have not been brought together previously. The difference between a 'notion' and a 'concept' was defined by Tim McGinty as follows;

> *Concepts are the antithesis of notions, which do not make any pretense [sic] about being appropriate. A notion for the design of a bird cage at a zoo might be that of a bird in flight. The fact that the design might not have enough unobstructed space in it to actually allow the birds to fly and get the exercise they need would be of no concern. As a notion the idea would be acceptable and perhaps amusing; as a concept, it would not be appropriate. A concept implies appropriateness; it supports the main intentions and goals of the project and respects each project's unique characteristics and restrictions. (McGinty, 1979, p. 212)*

A well thought out concept can, therefore, be a starting point, and one that we will return to later. Many design processes have been identified by those who have studied the way we think and those who research design methods. Some of the processes are complicated or do not suit every design problem, but it is worth looking at some of them.

An excellent explanation of these various procedures, and their development, has been made by Peter Rowe (Rowe, 1991, pp. 39–113). There are design procedures that follow a logical sequence, and generally consist of the following stages:

Preparation

Incubation

Illumination or Inspiration

Verification or Testing

The steps in this procedure were considered to be firmly progressive, feed-back loops between the steps were not considered. The so-called 'Iconic Model' that developed later did incorporate feed-back between the stages, but, as is pointed out by Rowe, it was strongly related to the earlier models and assumed that the solution would follow once the problem had been clearly defined.

THE ICONIC MODEL:

Analysis

Synthesis

Evaluation

Communication

A further modification to this was made by Bruce Archer (Archer, 1963–64) which in effect added feed-back stages at certain points:

Training

Brief Programming Experience

Data Collection

Analysis

Synthesis

Development

Communication

Solution

Linear processes such as these appear to deny the 'Eureka!' effect – that marvellous moment when the problem seems to solve itself. Some would have us believe that such a moment only happens to those who have the magical gift of 'creativity'. There are even those who regard the 'gift' as being exclusively given to creative architects; thus denying the breakthrough in scientific research in people like Watson and Crick (DNA) and even Archimedes himself. And yet we have all experienced it at some time, and careful observations of some animals, particularly squirrels raiding a bird table, would make us realize that it is not an exclusive human quality either.

Edward de Bono, (de Bono, 1971), is of the opinion that creativity is what he calls 'lateral thinking' and that it is contrary to the logical, sequential pattern of thinking. It is, put simply, a different way of looking at things. Despite that feeling of 'Eureka!' the problem did not solve itself of course. It required the collection of data first and, probably a lot of what de Bono calls 'vertical' thinking, i.e. a logical thought process. The creative jump takes you sideways out of the logical sequence to solve the problem, and in all probability will be a small part of the whole process. Thomas Edison, the famous inventor and no stranger to creative ideas, once said: 'Genius is one per cent inspiration and ninety-nine per cent perspiration.'

The explanation of the sequential method of problem solving given so far is, of course, oversimplified. In use there are many points at which there are feed-back loops and the action will go on on several fronts. Learning the skills of designing is sometimes like being an apprentice juggler. At first you are expected to juggle with three objects and just when you have mastered them you are thrown another; this process continues – it seems, at times, for ever.

However, let us go back to that elusive beginning, where the design process starts, and look at alternative methods which are not founded on the assumption that once the problem is defined the solution will follow on in sequential steps.

Experimental psychologists and those who research into design methodology, are of the opinion that when designers are faced with a problem they first of all re-structure it. This is not to say that there is an attempt to define the problem; it is, rather, an attempt to make it more understandable by re-structuring it, looking at it in different ways or breaking it down into its constituent parts and searching for some pattern in the relationship of those parts. This understanding may be furthered by testing a series of possible solutions against the context of the problem. The tentative solutions are therefore heuristic in nature, that is they prompt a possible way forward and form part of a generate and test procedure which helps towards learning about the problem and contributes to the search for a satisfactory solution.

These heuristic devices will largely depend upon earlier personal experience. However, they may also be acquired by the study of precedent using building types as models of a typology, or the application of the formal language of architectural form, and also certain recommendations and constraints. Such starting off points have been classified by Rowe as: 'anthropometric analogies, literal analogies, environmental relations, typologies and formal languages.' (Rowe, 1991, p. 80)

If we now go back to the quotation by Tim McGinty you will see that the notion of a bird in flight is a 'literal analogue'. It is, however, a notion or wild idea that, when tested against the true needs of the captive birds, does not work. But, it may serve its purpose as a heuristic in that it helps the designer to understand the problem better and may suggest the next step.

Rowe's classification 'environmental relations' is a fact-based analogy which makes use of the scientific principles underpinning the design of the built environment. It relates the possible solution to the site climate, the needs of the future occupants of the building and possibly the availability of natural resources to fulfil that need. Designing with a respect for climate is of this classification, as is the concept of the 'natural building' (which we will discuss in more detail later) and the desire to design energy efficient buildings. Its use will determine the orientation and shape of the building, and these characteristics will have to be tested against the available space on site and the building's function.

Architectural design owes much to history, and the study of architectural precedent can provide a means of studying a problem of today. Rowe makes a distinction between 'typologies and formal language', both of which are bound up with the analysis of precedent; but the main difference between the two may be seen as being that the former involves the application of the results of study, while the other is a given rule to be followed. There is a further blurring of the edges to be seen elsewhere in this classification of heuristics and it is possible to think of extensions to the groups covered by Rowe. Where, for instance, does the idea of 'spirit of place' fit? Obviously the main thing is not to worry about what to call these prompts, but

simply to use whatever you find most suited to the problem at hand. If you find that either yourself or the problem is best suited to this method of restructuring, rather than defining the problem, then you must realize that these heuristics are often only starting off points; they may need to be discarded so that better solutions are revealed. It is all too easy to take comfort in the adage that 'first thoughts are the best thoughts' and not to explore any alternative ideas.

It is important to remember that you are looking for a solution to a problem and not the other way around. Sometimes the designer's preferred solution resembles that flip line 'The answer is "Yes". What was the question?'. It is not always easy to abandon a designed solution, especially when you have invested so much of yourself in it, but it is important to know when to let it go. There are any number of existing buildings which neither suit their stated purpose nor their urban context, the designers apparently having had at some stage a ready-made solution which they have applied to the problem regardless of suitability. Design is perhaps too often thought of as a problem-solving activity, but as Dana Cuff's enquiry into the education and practice of architects showed, the necessary skill is 'sense making' (Cuff, 1991, p. 254). She agreed with Forrester's opinion about the work of architects and planners that 'If form giving is understood more deeply as an activity of making sense together, designing may then be situated in a social world where meaning, often multiple, ambiguous, and conflicting, is nevertheless a perpetual practical accomplishment.' (Forrester, 1985, p. 14)

It is often said that there are as many design methods as there are designers. While this is no doubt an exaggeration you will find that the same method does not help with every problem; you should keep an open mind and try different ways through the often tangled web of design.

This has been an overview of design methodology, much more has been written about the subject; should you wish to study it further you will find a number of sources in the list of Further Reading. Next we will consider, in outline at first, those heuristics and conceptual strategies that are particularly relevant to this book.

CLIMATE AS A DESIGN STRATEGY

The recommendation to 'design with the climate' may be considered as being both a heuristic, to get you started, and after testing the concept, a design strategy to follow throughout the design process. With today's concerns about the destruction of the ozone layer, the concept is now being seen as being particularly relevant. Site climate and the topology of the site are strongly linked, the one often being the cause of the other, and therefore the shape of the landscape may also suggest the built form; the long, low lines of many buildings confirm the idea.

It is possible to identify a respect for the site climate in vernacular style buildings, especially where the local climate is extreme and traditional building methods are still strong. A respect for climate is, of course, not the only influence on such buildings; a limited range of materials and their traditional use, religion, traditional building methods and culture may carry greater weight. Where climate is an important factor, however, the built form will be quite particular to its region. For example, in a hot, dry climate the building will be of a massive construction, the windows will be small and rarely opened during the day; the aim being to exclude the adverse climate, or at least slow down the effect of the baking hot sun. On the other hand, a hot, humid climate will generate the opposite response; the building will be light in weight with many openings to capture the benefit of the lightest breeze and its roof will overhang the walls to discharge the downpour of torrential rain.

Reyner Banham (1969) classified these two extremes of a response to climate as being the 'Conservative' mode of environmental management, suited to the hot, dry climate, and the 'Selective' mode to be found in the hot humid climate. It should be realized that these academic classifications do represent extremes of a response and a mixture of the components is more likely to be found where the climate is less adverse. Much has been written about designing with climate, its study is worthwhile and many of the books are quite delightful to read – if sometimes verging on the notion of nature as a religion, and you will find them in the list of Further Reading. We will consider the more pragmatic application of the principle and examine today's adoption and adaptation of the concept in more detail in the next chapter.

However, it is necessary to remind ourselves that the constituent parts of the local climate are more than those that are generated by natural means, in that air and noise pollution are often a more significant part of the problem on an urban site. It is a cliché to say that 'problems offer opportunities for creative solutions'. Nevertheless it is a cliché born of experience, as many architectural practices have demonstrated, and one such example is the subject of the case study of Briarcliff House, Farnborough.

In this instance the architects were Arup Associates of London, and they demonstrated their particular flair for showing that in the right hands the cliché is not simply something tutors tell their students. They were asked to design an office on an urban site, which was situated, more or less, on top of an existing shopping mall, itself not being of the highest quality. The shape of the site was determined by a road that curves around the southward-facing edge and the collection of buildings to the north. In addition to the noise from that road there is a four lane highway to the east and also an airport close by. Constraints such as the tightness of the site and the existing buildings to the north meant that the major part of the front elevation had to wrap around the southward perimeter. Vehicular noise and the possibility of excessive solar gain were therefore major problems. Arup's solution was to develop a deep buffer space which wraps around the U-shaped elevation, serving to attenuate both noise and the solar gain. However, the glazing system goes further than being a buffer space, it also captures some of the solar gain from that space and feeds this into the building's air-conditioning system and in addition provides a service zone for the the ducts which carry the conditioned air. The solution was said to have 'realized the environmental potential of the clichéd, fully glazed office facade' (Nelson, 1984). The building and its services are covered in more detail in one of the case studies that follow. In the analysis of that particular design the site climate and its pollutants were seen as strong constraints. However, they were also seen as a heuristic in that they prompted a re-arrangement of the problem, which in turn led to the innovative design of an office.

ENERGY CONSERVATION AS A DESIGN STRATEGY

Most of us are now aware of the need to conserve the Earth's natural resources. This concern has been brought more sharply into focus by the realization that burning fuel to produce electricity or simply to heat a building is causing damage to the protective ozone layer. An awareness such as this could promote an idea for a starting point for the design process.

An energy conscious design strategy will contain aspects of the 'design with climate' process in that it will involve an appreciation of the potential use of the site's ambient energy. However, it need not be the same strong determinant of the built form, for it is possible to design an energy efficient building that looks like any other; apart from a glass box disguised as a building, that is. It should be regarded as the all-purpose heuristic; the thread running through all future designs. Was it Mies who said that 'God is in the details'? He probably cared more about the purity of his style than the future of the world but a parody of his aphorism may be applied to the energy efficient building: 'energy efficiency is in the details'. It is also in the integration with the design of the environmental control systems, and we will turn our attention to all of this in a later chapter.

CONCEALED POWER AS A DESIGN STRATEGY

The title for this section is taken from *The Architecture of the Well-Tempered Environment* by Reyner Banham (1969), which is well worth seeking out since it is both informative and very readable. Banham's title refers to the ways in which the air-conditioning systems and their pipes and ducts, the presence of which made some buildings in the USA possible to work in, were concealed. The book goes on to show how the hatred that Louis Kahn, the

American architect, had for such things pushed him into designing a unique solution. Before we look at what he did, however, it is only right to point out that Frank Lloyd Wright recognized the problem before Kahn and solved it in a not too dissimilar fashion.

Lloyd Wright's problem was with the design of the Larkin Administration Building in Buffalo, New York State, which, incidentally, he claimed to be 'one of the first air-conditioned buildings in the country'. In point of fact it was not truly air-conditioned, not that that affects the point about to be made, and we will find out later why it was not. You may know that the building was, according to Banham, a 'vast vessel of space ringed by balconies' (Banham, 1969, p. 90) and that Lloyd Wright was inspired by the need to allocate space for the ventilation ducts to design the building with four towers, one at each corner, and that these served not only as stair towers, but also as the means of introducing air into the office spaces. Rather than being simply concealed, the ducts became part of the statement made by Lloyd Wright, Fig. 1.1.

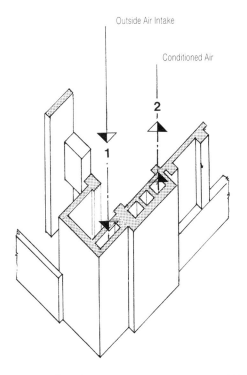

FIGURE 1.1 THE LARKIN BUILDING: CUT-AWAY SECTION OF SERVICES AND STAIR TOWER (AFTER BANHAM)

Kahn's problem, although materially similar, was, to a certain extent, self-imposed in that he saw the servicing system as an intrusion and a hated nuisance. Whether his hatred existed before he was commissioned to design the Richards Memorial Laboratories, Philadelphia, USA, is not recorded, but it must have reached a high point when he hit the problem of designing such a heavily serviced building. As a solution to the problem he conceived the idea of the building having two discrete parts, the 'Served' and the 'Servant' spaces; almost the same as the large houses in Britain which had back stairs for the servants so that the 'gentry' need not come in contact with them. Kahn gave those hated ducts and pipes a space of their own in towers outside the building proper and, instead of being merely hidden away, they too became part of the architectural statement, Fig. 1.2. It is sad to report that the idea was not entirely successful because it went astray once the services actually entered the 'served' spaces, but it has to be said that the fault was not entirely due to Kahn. Unfortunately the building did not provide the best built environment either, since many of the laboratories suffered from too much solar gain; a not too uncommon fault with the Modernists and their closet followers of today.

Can the idea of concealed power be considered as a heuristic? Did Kahn's dislike suggest a re-structuring of the problem? The function of the building most certainly called for a complex services system and therefore the hated, but necessary, ducts and pipes were the cause of the architectural articulation. And Lloyd Wright said that the form of the Larkin building was inspired by the need to allocate space for the air ducts. The answer is not important. In the hands of the creative designer, re-structuring the problem prompts the way ahead and it does not truly matter what we call the prompt. These last sections have picked out only those starting points which are most relevant to the subject of the book, and which will be developed in subsequent chapters. Obviously it would be possible to become more deeply involved in design methodology. However, the intention was to get the reader, and to some extent the writer also, started on the design process. The building you design will be all the better if you integrate your thoughts about

its developing form with those about allocating space for all those ducts and pipes, which Kahn hated so much.

There is no single perfect way of doing everything you need to do during the design process. Heath discovered that he could solve design problems in an orderly way and evolved an algorithm for the design of office buildings, but found that the same method could not be applied successfully to other types of buildings (Heath, 1984). He admits to being baffled and wondering that 'either there was no method for any type of design or one method must work for all designs'. (The 'one-method' attitude to design is what I regard as the 'Holy Grail' solution.) Heath realized that there is no one single method; however, he also realized that there are not as many methods as there are problems. His work brought him to the belief that design processes fall into three main classes and that within them there are many

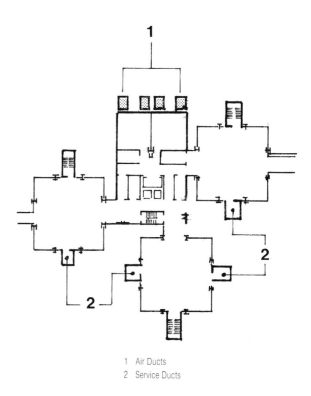

1   Air Ducts
2   Service Ducts

FIGURE 1.2 RICHARDS MEMORIAL LABORATORIES

variants. If Heath's theories are correct then their application could save you a lot of design time and you may like to test them.

We will follow a way as the book unfolds and it will tend to be problem-orientated because that is the nature of this particular study, but it is worth bearing in mind the warning given by Christopher Alexander in a retrospective preface to the paperback edition of his book *Notes on the Synthesis of Form* (Alexander, 1971): 'No one will become a better designer by blindly following this method, or indeed by following any method blindly.'

CHAPTER TWO

HEURISTICS IN USE

HEURISTICS AND THE BUILT FORM

A building can make a positive statement about energy conservation by recognizing and using to advantage the natural elements that surround it. Such a building will complement its environment, and do so in every portion and operation of the built systems.

   Richard G. Stein, 1977

In the first chapter we considered the concept of 'design with climate' as a starting off point, but recognized that it was not always a strong determinant of the built form. However, Stein's viewpoint is that a respect for the climate is firmly tied to the aim of conserving energy by building design; at the time of his statement interest in energy conservation had been awakened by the so-called 'energy crisis' of 1973. That interest should now have intensified into an active concern about the ever-growing impact we are making, not just upon natural resources, but also on the ozone layer. The cause of ozone depletion, and the effect it will have on all life forms, is now well documented and the generation of electrical power for use in buildings is a prime suspect. That threat may be lessened if buildings are made less dependent upon environmental control systems, particularly air-conditioning, and are designed to make use of the beneficial elements of the climate that surrounds them. If we are to do this it means taking a fresh look at the adage of 'design with climate'.

DESIGN WITH CLIMATE

Design with climate was considered as both a heuristic and possible generator of form in the previous chapter, and Reyner Banham's classifications of the Conservative and Selective modes as alternative responses to a particular climate were introduced (Banham, 1969). The response in each case took the form of a vernacular building, the construction of which was both an art and a science, and any rules for it were traditional and accepted rather than rationalized. Banham's classification was subsequently redefined by Dean Hawkes in an effort to both up-date it and make it more relevant to the design of energy conserving buildings, (Hawkes, 1982). Hawkes's modification is based upon the previous classification, but it is biased toward a greater understanding of the thermal interaction of the climate and the built form. It combines certain features of the earlier Selective and Conservative modes into a newly defined Selective mode. Hawkes also redefined another of Banham's modes, the Regenerative. This represents a mixture of both the previous Selective and Conservative modes. Banham saw the Regenerative mode as being less polarized than the other two and one that was more likely to be seen in common use. It relies less on its built form and incorporates the use of generated energy. Hawkes's modified Selective mode is identified as the design of the built form that admits those elements of the ambient climate which are beneficial, while keeping out those which are not, and which has a constructional mass that acts as a thermal flywheel to smooth out any peaks in the variations in temperature. The newly named Exclusive mode, does not make beneficial use of the site climate by the design of its built form, depending more upon generated energy, and therefore its form is most likely to be generated by considerations other than that of the site climate and the need to conserve energy.

Ideally a building designed in the Selective mode of environmental management will, therefore, be seen to sit upon its site at one with the climate, giving access to those phenomena of climate that are beneficial to the occupants, and denying access to those that are not. The overall effect would be to lessen the ecological impact created by the building and its occupants, and, in addition, it would provide pleasant internal and external spaces.

Alternatively, a building that is designed to exclude and ignore the site and its climate would be totally out of tune with its surroundings, giving the impression that its designer never left the comfort of the office and gained no inspiration from the context of the site. The building would be heavily dependent upon its building services to provide an acceptable indoor environment and be a greater, rather than less, threat to the world's ecology.

It should be realized that, like Banham's classification, the revised modes represent an idealistic academic strategy of design and are unlikely to exist in practice, but they are good models that may suggest a possible shape to the building at the beginning of the design process.

The design principles of the Selective mode are also referred to as Passive Design, and tend to be in sympathy with the concept of what has been called the Natural or Bioclimatic building.

THE NATURAL OR BIOCLIMATIC BUILDING

When Frank Lloyd Wright used the title *The Natural House* he meant that it was integral to its site, its environment and to the life of the inhabitants (Lloyd Wright, 1954). More recently the word 'natural' has been imbued with almost spiritual connotations, some adherents of the 'natural is good' concept of design apparently not realizing that at least a

passing acquaintanceship with some building science is necessary for success. The alternative title, 'Bioclimatic', comes from the German *Baubiologie*, or building biology, which in itself implies an application of science. Too often the writers of books on the subject tend to make the bucolic past something to return to, instead of an experience to be learnt from. In their books words like 'clean' and 'natural' become synonymous, conveniently forgetting that a well ordered septic tank is most certainly natural, but can it be considered as being clean?

Putting aside my personal prejudices about the over-estimated value of things just because they are said to be natural, I recognize that the 'natural' building offers many advantages; it will have a low environmental impact and should avoid the problem of the sick building syndrome. Properly designed, it should be the way ahead, but the principles of its design need to be understood and the limitations of their application to all possible building types realized. There is a risk of thinking that the design of such a building is simplistic and even benefits from its designer's lack of knowledge of building science. In point of fact its architecture is highly sophisticated, calling for greater rather than less knowledge of what makes the building work.

If the natural building is to be as independent, as is possible, of environmental control systems, including electric lighting, then it must be daylit and naturally ventilated. To limit the need for heating, it should give controlled access to sunshine, be well insulated and its constructional mass should play a part in providing human comfort. This being so, then its designer must have a working knowledge of designing for daylight, sunlight and natural ventilation and understand the role of the constructional mass. This knowledge will inform the design process as you move back and forth between the problem, the site climate and the concept of, in this case, the 'natural building'.

Before we start, however, it has to be said that this is not meant to be an exhaustive explanation of building science; it is more like a check list with some supporting explanation. There will be a need to do a fair amount of background reading, and the reading list is there to help you do just that. The whole of the book has been arranged so that you may find instant help quickly, but that you may also go into the subject in greater depth should you so wish.

Gaining the knowledge you need for each problem you encounter is not unlike peeling an onion, you can stop at the layer which suits your present need, but by going on down the layers you understand the basis for the rules of thumb that you use and the limitations of that use. It is fair to say that peeling onions can also cause tears.

ANALYSIS OF SITE CLIMATE

It seems pretty obvious that if the building is to be designed to be sympathetic with the climate then there is a definite need to know something about the climate on the site. A designer of such a building should at least have an understanding of those aspects that will have an effect upon the building, and yet sometimes some designers do not even know where the sun is with respect to the building they are designing.

It is not always possible to obtain detailed information about the site climate, because data that is reliable needs to be collected over a long period of time, otherwise it is simply a snapshot of the weather and not climatic data. What is the difference between weather and climate? It is said that 'Weather is something we have to put up with, the climate is something we measure'.

However, failing sufficient reliable information about the climate on site to make a proper analysis possible, it is often enough to know something of the topography and how it would change the regional climate to that which is experienced on site. It is easier to discover data about the regional climate in most developed countries, either from the Meteorological Office in the UK or its equivalent elsewhere; local airports can also be very helpful, but be warned some countries regard climatic data as being security sensitive.

In the context of this book we may limit our study and only consider solar radiation, wind movement, air temperature and humidity. There are various design tools to help us to move from the regional data to that of the site area. Some of them will enable us to visualize the position of the sun with respect to the site, while others will suggest how the patterns of air movement may develop over it, given some basic information about the topography. It is also possible to estimate the air temperature that is likely to prevail during any two-hour period in the day from the average monthly maximum and minimum temperatures.

THE PATH OF THE SUN AND SOLAR RADIATION

We need to understand the apparent movement of the sun with respect to the site for several reasons. First, if it is intended to utilize the solar heat gain then access for sunshine into the building must be designed, whether it is simply a window, an atrium or a solar collection device, and this can only be done effectively if the position of the sun in the sky is known. Secondly, we must be able to design against too much sun to prevent overheating and glare. And finally, sunlight can be a delight both inside and outside the building, and its pleasing effect can be optimized if we relate the building to the sun's path. The movement of the sun can be plotted on what are known as 'Sun Path Diagrams'. These show the path of the sun as projected on a horizontal, two-dimensional plane, Fig. 2.1. Using the diagram it is possible to determine the position of the sun hour by hour throughout the year.

Shadows will be cast on the site by the natural topography, trees and other vegetation, together with any other buildings that already exist. This may be a disadvantage during the heating season in a cold climate, but just the opposite during periods of overheating. There are various ways of determining

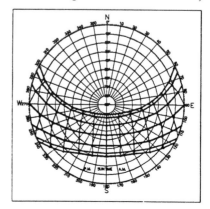

FIGURE 2.1 SUN PATH DIAGRAM

the times when the sun's rays are blocked from reaching the site; some of these are illustrated by Mazria (Mazria, 1979, p. 290) and by Brown (Brown, 1985, p. 14). In passing it is worth pointing out that the building you are designing will, if built, also cast its own shadow and in so doing could restrict solar access to another building. Although this is presently only of academic interest in the UK it has assumed greater importance in the USA where there are City Ordinances that protect solar access (in some ways these are similar to the protection given by 'Ancient Lights' in the UK). Tabb outlines three methods of determining what is called 'solar zoning' (Tabb, 1984, p. 84).

When the obstructions have been plotted it is possible to model the periods of solar access and, if need be, develop and test solar shading devices. There are several ways of testing a model, the simplest of which involves the use of a matchbox size sundial. This is more for fun than accuracy, and should not be used for a serious study. A polar sundial together with a good spotlight mounted a good distance away from the model will provide the basis for a more accurate study. The most familiar method, and one that provides a good degree of accuracy for the effort involved, is the heliodon (Koenisberger et al, 1973, p. 269). There are also now available several computer programs that facilitate the study. These do have the usual advantages of computer simulation, but are not always cheap to buy and operate.

WIND MOVEMENT

Wind movement around a building can be both a benefit and a nuisance. It is the prime cause of natural ventilation, but also the cause of heat loss and the wrecking of plans for social spaces outdoors. As designers we need to know the direction of the wind and its speed at different seasons of the year; if you plan to use wind-powered electricity generators this knowledge is essential.

Two prime sources of this information are available: the *CEC European Wind Atlas* (Troen & Peterson, 1989) and *WMO Technical Note* 175, 'Meteorological aspects of the utilisation of wind as an energy source' (WMO, 1981). The data in the *Wind Atlas* is excellent but not readily available.

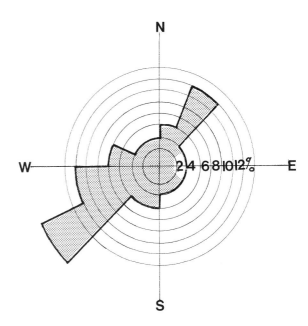

FIGURE 2.2 TYPICAL WIND ROSE

There is a guide to its use in *Energy in Architecture: The European Passive Solar Handbook* (Goulding et al, 1993, pp. 20–35).

It is possible to determine the velocity, direction and frequency of the wind over a region from what is known as the 'wind rose'. Although the wind rose can be illustrated in more than one way the most informative is that shown in Fig. 2.2. It is worth remembering that the given direction of the wind refers to where it is coming from; hence a 'south-westerly wind' is coming from the south-west.

The regional data is almost certain to come from a weather station some distance from the site, and its speed and direction will have been modified by the terrain the wind has covered before it arrives. When the wind moves over the ground its speed and direction will be modified by the roughness of the surface. Vegetation, trees and buildings contribute to the roughness and they slow down the air as it passes over and through them. At some distance above these obstructions the wind increases in velocity at a constant value until it is no longer affected by them; the region so affected is called the 'boundary layer'. The roughness is categorized descriptively as being, flat open land or sea, rough woodlands and urban, and the wind velocity over a zone is assumed to obey a simple power law. It is

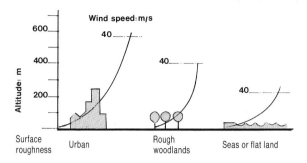

FIGURE 2.3 WIND SPEED GRADIENT

usual to illustrate the affect on the wind speed as a gradient, Fig. 2.3.

Although it will be difficult to determine the air's modified speed and direction when it arrives on site, it is possible to get a good idea of the pattern of air movement by knowing something about the effect of the topography, Fig. 2.4. In my experience the actual measurement of the wind speed over a site is fraught with difficulties, the use of hand-held anemometers tells you more about the sense of humour of the teacher than the features of the wind. If it is necessary to determine what it is, then it is best left to the experts, but do not expect a quick answer if you want accuracy. In the majority of cases it is sufficient to understand how the wind moves across the site and how it behaves when it meets an obstruction like the building. Knowing that, you can then plan entrances, outdoor social spaces and the openings needed for natural ventilation with confi-

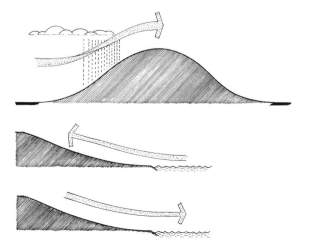

FIGURE 2.4 TOPOGRAPHY AND WIND PATTERN

dence. If you have the resources of a wind tunnel, even a small one can inform the design if its limitations are understood, then more is possible, and for very exposed sites with the possibility of heavy snow fall its use is essential.

In the 1960s too many designers produced shopping centres coupled with blocks of flats that together produced minor whirlwinds; there were even a number of deaths caused when older people were blown over by the wind between the buildings. If you are planning outdoor spaces take care with the spatial relationship of the buildings for this reason. There is now sufficient information available to prevent such ill-informed designs happening again (Penwarden, 1975).

AIR TEMPERATURE AND HUMIDITY

The ambient air temperature is influenced by the topography, the nature of the vegetation and that of the ground surfaces, any nearby mass of water and, in an urban situation, the other buildings. The phenomena known as 'heat islands' that are created in cities have been studied by several people; these are localized zones where the temperature is higher than the surrounding area, and are the result of the hard surfaces storing heat, and the wind effects. Chandler showed that the climate within a city is likely to be about 10% more temperate than that of the surrounding rural areas (Chandler, 1965). Of course, some cities also suffer because of the effect buildings have on the climate, especially if the buildings are multi-storey. Chicago earned its title of the 'Windy City' at the expense of its inhabitants' discomfort; in the winter the skyscrapers there bring the colder air above the city down to pavement level in mind-numbing blasts.

Any decision about the adoption of the Bioclimatic building design mode must be informed by a knowledge of the prevailing temperature, in particular its maximum and minimum, and compared with acceptable comfort levels. Later on in this chapter we will consider a design aid by Givoni which brings together a knowledge of climate and comfort levels so that an environmental design strategy may be formed. It is possible to begin to formulate some idea of such a strategy if the outdoor temperatures are known, and this can be done starting from the basis of the monthly maximum and minimum temperatures.

The study of the climate as applied to building design is a must as we move towards an energy deficient future and this explanation only scratches the surface. The climate affects every part of building design; the structure, the choice of materials and the way they are put together must be informed by a knowledge of it.

Designing buildings for people is not easy, and trying to ensure that both the building and the environmental control system come together to provide a place that is a pleasure to be in demands a knowledge of the climate and the standards of comfort that the occupants expect. It has been suggested that the purpose of the building may be regarded as a climatic filter, standing between the climate on one side and the expectations of the occupants on the other. This is far too simplistic a view of what the building is about, but it is a neat summary of the way in which we should approach the design of the natural building.

HUMAN COMFORT AND WARMTH

We have reviewed those aspects of the climate that demand our attention and now we must look at the other part of the equation, that which makes people feel comfortable and warm. This knowledge will form part of the information needed if we are to test the design concept. Understanding the climate is the easier part, pleasing every one of the occupants is not only difficult, it has been proven scientifically to be impossible: 'He [Swope] enunciated no rules for success, but offered a sure formula for failure: "Just try to please everyone."' (E.J. Kahn Jr.)

Comfort is a subjective sensation; however, there are some measurable contributory factors to the sensation and it is these that give credence to the principles that underpin the design of the built environment, and in particular the design of environmental control systems. The feeling of human comfort and warmth, better described as a feeling of wellbeing, depends on six identifiable factors, the first four of which are part of the built environment,

while the remaining two depend upon the actions of the individual occupant. These are:

● Ambient air temperature
● Air velocity
● Relative humidity
● Temperature of the room's surfaces (the area weighted value of which is described as Mean Radiant Temperature)
● Metabolism and therefore the activity of the occupant
● Clothing and therefore the thermal insulation it provides for the occupant

In both voluntary and involuntary ways we attempt to maintain a balance in the rate at which heat is transferred to and from our body. The aim being to maintain a deep body temperature of about 37 degrees C. This we do to survive as well as to maintain that sense of wellbeing. When there is an equal balance in the rate of heat output to input, then the experience of comfort and warmth is said to be at its maximum.

METABOLIC RATE AND ACTIVITY

Of all the energy produced by the human body about 80% is dissipated in some form of heat to the environment that surrounds it. The rate at which this heat energy is produced is a function of activity; the harder the body works the greater the production and vice versa. This rate is known as the 'Metabolic Rate' and is related to the surface area of the body, the unit adopted is the 'met'; one met being equal to a heat output of 58 W/m^2, it being assumed that the average area of the body is 1.8 square metres. Typically a person sitting would produce 1 met, but someone dancing would produce a far higher rate of 3 to 5 met.

CLOTHING AND HEAT OUTPUT

Apart from its social and fashion value, clothing also provides the body with insulation against the gain and loss of heat. This effect is expressed as a thermal resistance and, like that of the met, the unit has a curious name – the 'clo' and is equal to 0.155 $\text{m}^2 \text{ K/W}$. And to give you some idea of its value, a lounge suit, shirt etc. provides 1 clo and shorts, lightweight shirt etc. between 0.3 to 0.4 clo.

COMFORT AND AIR MOVEMENT

Air movement can be either a contributor to our comfort or a nuisance; it depends upon our own condition, our level of activity and the temperature, velocity and moisture content of the moving air. If our rate of activity is high and there is a need for evaporative cooling to ensure comfort, then higher air velocities would be welcomed. Conversely, a low air temperature coupled with a high wind speed will cause great discomfort, this combined effect is called the 'wind chill factor' and at its most severe poses a direct threat to survival.

In an indoor environment, that combined effect will only be felt as an annoying draught, but still be sufficient to cause discomfort and complaints. The direction of the air movement with respect to an occupant is also important, it being argued that the back of the neck and the ankles are particularly sensitive to air movement, although it is said that air movement felt on the forehead is generally experienced as a welcome cooling effect (Markus & Morris, 1980, p. 63). These simple facts can be most usefully employed when designing an auditorium and deciding on the relationship between the arrangement of the seating and that of the incoming supply air from the ventilation system. It is obviously better to ensure that the air moves towards the audience, and, if this is not possible, to keep the air velocity below acceptable limits. See also Chapter Ten, the Design Exercise for an auditorium, and Chapter Fifteen, the Case Study of the Concert Hall.

INDICES OF THERMAL COMFORT

As has been explained already, human comfort depends upon several parameters, and the measurement of only one of them cannot be expected to give a reliable indication of acceptable conditions. Many researchers have sought for a way of measuring the combined effect of those parameters and relating it to a thermal index of human comfort. The research started well over a century ago. Markus makes mention of observations made by Arbuthnot in 1733 and also the development later in 1804 by Sir John Leslie of a modification to the simple thermometer to enable him to measure air velocity (Markus & Morris, 1980, p. 37).

More than 50 of these thermal indices have been developed, many too limited to be accepted. More recently Houghten and Yaglou produced the 'Effective Temperature Scale' (ET) in 1923, but this ignored the effect of radiant heat and was subsequently improved by Bedford in 1940. Bedford (1940/1961) introduced the concept of mean radiant temperature and called the revised index the 'Corrected Effective Temperature' (CET).

'Operative Temperature' is an index that incorporates mean radiant temperature. It is defined as being the uniform temperature (air temperature being equal to mean radiant temperature) of an imaginary enclosure in which an occupant would exchange the same quantity of sensible heat by radiation and convection as in an actual environment. In environments where the air velocity is in the range 0.1–1.0 m/s this index has been shown to provide a reasonable approximation of the feeling of comfort or discomfort.

Humphreys has shown that the mean radiant temperature can be derived from measurements taken by a thermometer (or thermistor/thermocouple) in a 40 mm diameter blackened globe (Humphreys, 1975). It is even possible to use a simple blackened table tennis ball for the purpose. I have done so on several occasions and found the accuracy to be acceptable – especially under field work conditions. Later work by Gagge, supported by the American Society for Heating, Refrigeration and Air Conditioning Engineers (ASHRAE), produced an index that has found wide acceptance among practioners and is called the 'Standard Effective Temperature' (SET) (for a full discussion of SET and its use see Markus & Morris, 1980).

Recent field trials have shown the occupants of a fair cross-section of orthodox buildings to be comfortable at room temperatures lower than those predicted by laboratory-based research (Griffiths, 1990). Whereas thermal neutrality, using the accepted optimal operative temperature index, would have been predicted to be in the range 23–25 degrees C, it was found that the occupants were comfortable in the range 19–21 degrees C. The trials showed that these results also held good for buildings heated by means of passive solar systems, there being no real difference in the accepted temperature range. Growing interest in passive solar systems and the Bioclimatic concept has re-awakened interest in some work done by Humphreys as early as 1975 (Humphreys, 1975). He came to the conclusion, after studying data from several countries, that the neutral temperature could be predicted from the prevailing temperature outdoors. For example, if the monthly mean outdoor temperature is −1 degrees C in the winter and 22 degrees in the summer, then according to Humphreys the respective acceptable indoor temperatures would be 19 degrees C and 23 degrees C. If accepted as being suited to design in the 'real' world then this means that the energy demand for heating and cooling could be reduced. Work is also going ahead on thermal transients, where the conditions vary with time, and the increased feeling of personal alertness that such changes provide.

In brief, the environment we design can contribute to the well-being of the occupants of our building, every choice of the material of construction and where it is placed has an effect; that it is possible to measure the overall contribution of that environment, and to set standards of performance that we can work towards, but that the continuing application of those standards is being questioned and we need to know the answers because it could change the way we design.

BIOCLIMATIC CHARTS

Thermal indices may be used as a means of analysing the cause of discomfort in a room, or as the basis of the design criteria of an environmental control system, but in that they do not relate directly to the site climate they are not capable of giving guidance to the choice of an appropriate control strategy, particularly when the hope is to make use of ambient energy. An attempt to do this was first made by Olgyay (Olgyay, 1963). His 'Bioclimatic Chart' was meant to be a systematic aid to facilitate the design of a building that was sympathetic to the site climate and human comfort. However, Olgyay's chart is only based on the outdoor climate and not the conditions that would prevail indoors. Givoni pointed out that the chart made no allowance for the possible contribution to comfort that could be made by the building construction, and that

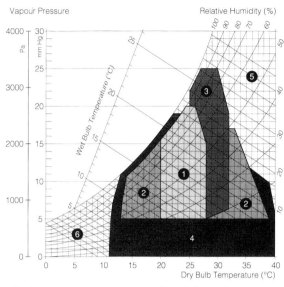

1 Comfort zone
2 Zone of influence of thermal inertia
3 Zone of influence of ventilation
4 Zone of influence of occupant behaviour
5 Air conditioning zone
6 Heating zone

FIGURE 2.5 GIVONI'S BIOCLIMATIC CHART

although it was partially applicable to a humid climate, it would lead to errors in decisions made for a hot arid region (Givoni, 1981, p. 311). Givoni therefore developed the 'Building Bioclimatic Chart'. This is based on his 'Index of Thermal Stress' and requires an analysis of the site climate. It provides guidance about the constructional features of the building and a possible environmental control strategy, Fig. 2.5. Mark lines connecting the mean maximum and minimum dry-bulb temperatures with the mean coincident wet-bulb temperatures for each month. Plot the resulting intersections for both maximum and minimum dry-bulb values. Connect these points to see which strategy zone each month falls in. The results will give you the basis for a possible strategy. The chart makes no allowance for internal heat gains which may need to be regulated with the use of an environmental control system.

GIVING FORM TO THE CONCEPT

At this point it is as well to stop and review the ground covered so far, and take stock. We have been assembling some knowledge, or perhaps revising some half-forgotten facts, and shaping it into a design tool that will help us test a heuristic. In our present case the heuristic is the concept of the natural building. The selection of that particular concept was made because it suited the central purpose of this book, and it is relevant to today's concern about the environment. We will consider other types of building later, and these too can be tested by the tools we have assembled so far.

Let us now begin to flesh out the shadowy form of the concept. There are some useful rules of thumb that can be used to begin to give shape to the building, or to check the shape being generated by other factors.

DAYLIGHTING

The depth of a room which may be considered as being daylit from a window, on one side of the room only, is equal to $2\frac{1}{2}$ times the height of the top of the window. In normal height rooms the effective depth of daylight is therefore 6 to 7 metres. The area of glass need not be large, 40 to 50% of the total area of 'walling' should be sufficient. High window placement in a room projects light into a room. For example, a window height of 2.25 metres will produce about 60% less illumination at the rear of a room than one having a height of 4 metres.

NATURAL VENTILATION

If a room can be daylit then it can be naturally ventilated, implying therefore that the same limitation to depth applies, i.e. 6 to 7 metres, unless there are openings in addition to those in one outside wall. The shape of a building and its orientation have a strong influence on the efficacy of natural ventilation. Effective ventilation requires an air inlet and outlet. Two openings in a wall are more effective than one having the same area.

SUNLIGHT AND ORIENTATION

Sunlight can be a blessing and a curse, its access into a building therefore needs to be controlled. In general if the window to walling ratio exceeds 45% on a south face then solar gain will prove to be excessive. There are two opposing rules:

If solar gain is wanted, the longest wall of the building should face south and the largest windows should be in that wall, but during the warmer months shading will be necessary, especially if the glass area is greater than 45% of the total area of walling.

If solar gain and glare is to be avoided, at latitudes greater than 45 degrees, then the building should be more square to minimize the south elevation, or turned away from the sun's path.

To minimize solar gain on or near the equator the east and west walls and the roof should be minimized in area. The opposite applies, more significantly the further away the building is from the equator.

HEAT TRANSFER (LOSS AND GAIN)

To minimize the heat transferred through the building fabric the enclosed volume should be high in relation to the exposed surface area. The shape should tend towards the compact. In general the heat loss of a building is about 25–30 W/m³ and the cooling load of a typical office is about 150 W/m³ for a perimeter zone and 75 W/m³ for an inner zone.

RULES OF THUMB AND THEIR USE

Rules of thumb can be used to generate ideas or to check them. They are not to be treated as if they were written in stone; indeed some rely more on myths and legends than scientific fact. In summary, rules of thumb can be helpful, but they should be used with care for there are limits to their application, even when, as those outlined above are, based upon scientific knowledge.

DESIGNING FOR DAYLIGHT

In a generally overcast sky, such as that which usually prevails in the UK, the light is diffuse, and it is at its brightest at the top of the vault of the apparent dome of the sky. It follows, therefore, that if a working surface in a room can 'see' more of that bright source than other such surfaces in the same room, then it will receive more light. The light that is incident on the surface is also made up of that which is reflected from all the other surfaces in the room, together with that which is reflected into the room off surfaces outside. We can extend this basic, somewhat over-simplified, explanation and derive

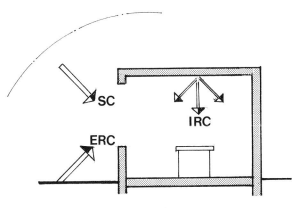

SC: Sky Component, direct from overcast sky
ERC: Externally Reflected Component, light reflected by external surfaces
IRC: Internally Reflected Component, light reflected by internal surfaces
DF = SC + ERC + IRC

FIGURE 2.6 DAYLIGHT FACTOR

the familiar concept of the Daylight Factor (DF). The DF is a ratio of the daylight illumination outdoors, compared simultaneously with that indoors, which is incident upon a certain point in a particular building. Fig. 2.6. shows the components of the mathematical expression.

Until recently it was usual in the UK to design for daylight with reference to a minimum daylight factor that was required at a particular point in a room; factors of between 1 to 2%, having been found to be acceptable, were the norm. It is now recommended by the Chartered Institute of Building Services Engineers (CIBSE) that the average daylight factor is a better basis for window design, and an average daylight factor of 5% or more is said to provide a cheerful daylit interior. For a complete guide to the design sequence you should see *CIBSE Applications Manual: Window Design*, 1987.

There are several ways of calculating the area of glass needed for a particular Daylight Factor (Szokolay, 1980, p. 126), and there are computer programs now available that not only do the tedious work, they also illustrate DF contours across the room. Perhaps the best design aid is the artificial sky that facilitates the testing of physical models (Moore, 1985, p. 175). However, at the strategic stage of the design it is possible to test the depth of the room for availability of daylight by using the nomogram shown on Fig. 2.7; it relates the geometry of the room to window area and Daylight Factor. In

this way we can explore the feasibility of the shape of the building and decide whether an alternative daylighting strategy is necessary. Later, when the design is firmer, it can be tested with the methods outlined above.

It will be obvious that no matter how large the window is, if the room is too deep and there is insufficient light then electric lighting will have to be used during the day. However, it is possible to improve the conditions by ensuring that the surfaces of the room, in particular the ceiling, are painted in light colours and kept clean so that they reflect the incoming light. Light shelves are often used under the mistaken impression that they will 'bounce' light off the ceiling so that it will penetrate further into the room. The shelf is placed in an intermediate position within the window system, dividing the upper and lower glazed areas, projecting partially outwards and partially inwards into the

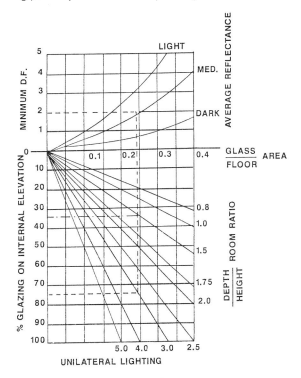

Example: enter for a DF of 2%, assume average reflectance is medium. Determine room geometry, assumed depth/height ratio is 3.0 and therefore glazed area needs to be 75%.

FIGURE 2.7 DAYLIGHTING NOMOGRAM (AFTER POOLE & BIRD)

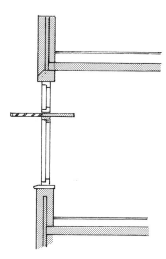

FIGURE 2.8 LIGHT SHELF, TYPICAL ARRANGEMENT

room, Fig. 2.8. Although there is some increase in the light reflected off the ceiling, in practice this is offset by a loss of sky light that is obstructed by the shelf. However, they do reduce sky glare close to the window and therefore contribute to a better, and more even, distribution of light throughout the room, Fig. 2.9. In addition, the projection outside serves a useful purpose, when fitted into a south facing window, in that it will reduce the solar radiation incident upon the window. Such uses were explored as a means of ensuring comfort for hospital patients by Hopkinson and Kay; they were designed as 'anti-glare baffles' rather than light shelves (Hopkinson & Kay, 1966, p. 533). However,

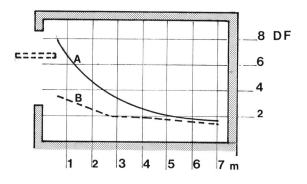

A: DF without light shelf   B: DF with light shelf

FIGURE 2.9 DAYLIGHT FACTOR, WITH AND WITHOUT LIGHT SHELF (AFTER FULLER MOORE)

Erno Goldfinger claimed to have invented the device, calling it the 'photobolic screen'. He incorporated it in the design for 46 Albermarle Street, London in 1955.

Light shelves will perform quite differently under bright sky conditions, when the light is more directional than when it is scattered from a diffuse sky. They have, for example, been used to good effect in the USA (Lam, 1983, pp. 95–7). Lam is of the opinion that they are useful for the distribution of sunlight with reduced glare. He gives as an extreme example that of the Lockheed building, Sunnyvale, California, the shelves of which are about 4 metres deep and are designed to project sunlight into the depth of the offices even when the windows are closed off by either blinds or the offices at the perimeter.

NATURAL VENTILATION

If only we could see the wind moving around buildings it would be a lot easier to understand how natural ventilation works, because designing for it is plagued by what may be called the 'intelligent arrow syndrome'. The intelligent arrow is the one that you often see on drawings, optimistically showing the air coming into a room the way the designer needs it to go. Unfortunately air follows the laws of science as defined by Newton and not wishful thinking; once it is on the move it will continue to go in its original direction until some external force re-directs it or it runs out of momentum; but more about this later.

A room will need to be ventilated for various reasons. There may be a need to remove or dilute foul or toxic gases, or to maintain the internal temperature at an acceptable level, or to effect direct cooling of the occupants. If this is to be done by natural ventilation then it must be realized that the effect will be variable because, obviously, the motivating forces that bring about the movement of air in a building are themselves as variable as the climate. These motivating forces are the wind pressure on the building and the so-called 'stack effect' due to the buoyancy of the air. They may work separately or in tandem, but generally speaking the wind is the strongest force of the two in the UK, and its effect depends on the relationship of its direction and the shape of the building.

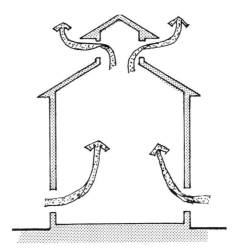

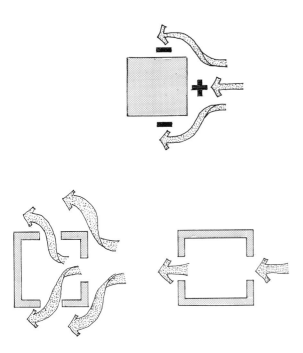

Cross-ventilation

FIGURE 2.11 THE 'STACK EFFECT'

FIGURE 2.10 PRESSURE ZONES AND WIND MOVEMENT

As the wind meets and moves around and over a building it develops zones which are of positive and negative pressures relative to each other. It is this difference in pressure, and where it occurs, that we can utilize to good effect, Fig. 2.10. Cross-ventilation can occur between a positive and a negative zone and, as can be seen from Fig. 2.10, the openings that allow the flow of air need not be directly opposite each other. For effective ventilation each ventilated space must have an air inlet and an outlet. (This is where the intelligent arrow comes in; if you haven't got both an inlet and outlet then the only solution is to draw an arrow to convince yourself that it will work, even though you now know that it will not.)

The motivating force of the stack effect is an increased buoyancy of the air due to an increase in temperature. For it to work, therefore, the incoming air must be cooler than that in the room, and the position of its inlet lower than that of the outlet, Fig. 2.11. Tall, British colonial style rooms with high and low openings are suited to the effect, or the atria — just so long as they conform with Fire Regulations.

Putting the two effects together by placing the outlet of the stack in the negative zone created by the wind flowing over the buildings will enhance both effects, Fig. 2.12. But be aware that the sum of the two is not equal to that of the two parts. As a rule of thumb assume the total effect to be no greater than the greater force + 10%.

Although there is no rule of thumb that relates the effectiveness of natural ventilation to the depth of a room, similar to that of the efficacy of daylighting, it

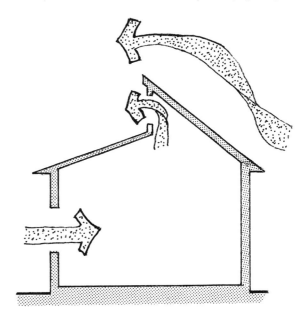

FIGURE 2.12 COMBINATION OF WIND PRESSURE & STACK EFFECT

is safe to say that if a room can be daylit, then it can be ventilated. Putting it another way, under normal conditions a room having a depth of no more than 6 to 7 metres can be naturally ventilated by an openable window in one of its sides. It must be realized, however, that it is not possible to reduce the temperature of a room below that of the air outside using natural ventilation alone. The occupants may be made more comfortable in such conditions if the incoming air comes in contact with them, because if the air is not too humid there will be an evaporative cooling effect. It is important to understand something about the way air moves into a room and its controlling factors.

It has been shown that, depending on the wind direction, in rooms with only one opening window the average air velocity is about 3.3 to 4.7% of the wind velocity, and that the window size has little effect (Givoni, 1981). Two openings in the same wall will improve matters, the average velocity then increasing to between 4.3 and 15.7%. Interestingly, if wings are added externally to the window openings and the wind blows obliquely to them, then the average velocity will increase to 35%, Fig. 2.13. (Givoni, 1981, p. 289).

The position and size of the air inlet and outlet determine the way in which air flows within the room, but partitions or other similar obstructions can block and deflect the air movement despite

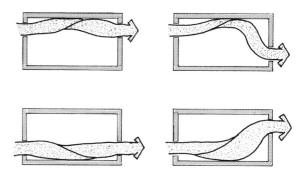

FIGURE 2.14 PATTERN OF AIR MOVEMENT AND POSITION OF ENTRY POINT

careful design of these. If the aim is to change the air in a room without the occupants being made aware of the movement, then it is best to have both inlet and outlet at high level, above the occupied zone. However, if contact cooling is necessary then obviously the openings must be within the occupied zone. Old-fashioned sash type windows are good in this respect because openings can be arranged at high or low level. In general, the position and size of the inlet opening is the greater determinant of the pattern of air movement, Fig. 2.14.

Much attention is presently being given to the design of naturally ventilated buildings, in order to reduce the dependence on mechanical ventilation and the use of electrical power. A benchmark for the design of a daylit and naturally ventilated building for a commercial client was put in place when Arup Associates designed the building known as Gateway Two for Wiggins Teape in Basingstoke. In its outward appearance it looks like other well-designed office buildings, less tall than its neighbouring Gateway One, but otherwise somewhat similar. However, unlike that neighbour, it is not air-conditioned even though the function is the same. Instead of the air-conditioning system the building works 'naturally'. An elegant, four-storey glazed central atrium, surrounded on all four sides by offices, introduces light into the core of the building and also serves as the 'pump' to provide natural ventilation. It is the natural way in which the building works that leads to the difference in height, as Dean Hawkes commented in an article for the *Architects'*

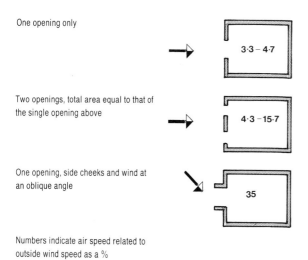

One opening only

3·3 – 4·7

Two openings, total area equal to that of the single opening above

4·3 – 15·7

One opening, side cheeks and wind at an oblique angle

35

Numbers indicate air speed related to outside wind speed as a %

FIGURE 2.13 AIR SPEED IN ROOMS (AFTER GIVONI)

Journal: 'the need to accommodate a full airconditioning system increases the floor to floor height of Gateway One so that it has only four storeys to Gateway Two's five' (Hawkes, 1983).

The stack effect, provided by the atrium, pulls in air through openable windows in the external wall, across the offices and through louvred windows into the central space. There is a simple low temperature hot water heating system supplying heat to the offices which can be controlled by the occupants, and the atrium has an underfloor heating system, the heat for which is supplied, indirectly, by the computers. Originally the designers placed an agreed limit to the proportion of cellular to open offices so as to ensure good cross-ventilation. Unfortunately, more recently a change in management structure has gradually eroded this arrangement and the size and number of cellular offices is increasing, to the detriment of the natural ventilation; so much so that desktop fans are now making an appearance.

Tall ventilation stacks are once more becoming a part of the architectural statement, similar to those designed by Waterhouse for the Natural History Museum, London in 1873. Waterhouse located a cast-iron chimney from the boilers in the north-west ventilation tower to produce an increased stack effect, whereas today's towers rely on solar power to provide a heating effect.

The new Engineering and Manufacturing School, de Montfort University, Leicester, is the latest design to adopt the principles of natural ventilation and to apply them to auditoria, classrooms and laboratories. Designed by the Short-Ford Partnership, it is based on physical and computer modelling techniques and utilizes only the combined effect of wind action and the pressure developed by tall 'solar' towers to provide effective ventilation. Air is drawn in, under the effect of the solar towers, directly from the streets surrounding the building through pierced brick walls and buttresses and, in the case of the lecture theatres, over heated coils before being introduced into the space below the seats. It is as yet too early to know how effective the design is; the principles are correct but success will largely depend on the occupants and their understanding of how the building is designed to work.

ORIENTATION AND SOLAR GAIN

Solar gain can be a benefit because, properly utilized, it can help to heat a building, but it can also be a nuisance. Le Corbusier aimed to provide the occupants of the Salvation Army hostel in Paris with the 'ineffable joy' of sunlight during the winter, and this he did by making the whole of its southerly elevation a wall of single glazing. According to Banham it worked well throughout the cold winter, but became increasingly uncomfortable as spring turned to summer. So much so that Le Corbusier had to invent the *brise-soleil*, or sunshade, soon afterwards. It is, like so many other ideas, necessary to find a balance and express it in the design, rather than trust to an inspired late modification (Banham, 1969, p. 157).

If we are to avoid making the same mistake and make good use of solar gain we must start by knowing where the sun is with respect to our proposed building at each significant time of the year. This is because the path of the sun varies with the seasons and the latitude, and the intensity of solar radiation incident upon any surface of a building is directly related to that path, and dependent upon the same variables. Solar path diagrams are a useful design aid and have been referred to earlier in this chapter. You should familiarize yourself with these diagrams and other aids such as the heliodon.

Following on from such a study it is possible to make decisions about orientation, the shape of the building, the location and size of windows and the possible need for shading. If the intention is to maximize solar gain, in the more northern climates, then obviously the building should have its axis running east to west, so that the glazed areas may receive the most intense radiation. This location for the glazing and its size should be considered in terms of the energy balance of the window. There is no real advantage in designing the largest glazed area possible because the glass will lose a great deal of heat during the colder months and there would be a negative energy balance for the whole year. Windows with different orientations will have their own energy balance, a north-facing window is more likely to have a negative balance than any on the other orientations.

It is far wiser to use glass as part of designing for daylight; its use reduces the need for electricity, and that is the main aim of any 'green' policy. Personal experience has shown that when designing windows it is better to 'start with the light', in this case daylight; get that right and considerations of passive solar features will follow.

CONSTRUCTIONAL MASS

In an energy efficient design strategy the mass of a building has many parts to play, apart from its traditional role of holding up the roof. It can be a heat sink that admits and stores heat from various sources, such as solar gain or the heat emitted by machines of various sorts and that given off by electric lights, together with that from the occupants. Or it can do just the opposite to good effect, being designed to be cooled down, usually when the building is unoccupied, by the introduction of cold night air, or be located so that it loses heat by radiation to the black vault of the sky at night. The ability to do all these things depends upon the material it is made from, the nature of its exposed surface and where it is located.

The materials that are traditionally used for the construction of buildings, concrete, brick and stone, all have thermal properties suited to the storage of heat. They are by nature dense, are able to rapidly transfer heat from their surfaces to the interior by virtue of a higher conductivity and have a high specific heat capacity which means that they have a good ability to store the heat they receive. These two properties need to be present in combination for, although some materials have a high heat capacity, they are not able to conduct heat. The comparison of brick and wood is a good example, both having similar specific heat capacities, but the former, being a better insulator than a conductor, has a much lower conductivity.

Material	Specific Heat Capacity (J/kg K)	Thermal Conductivity (W/m K)
Cast concrete	840	1.40
Wood, pine	1210	0.115

Materials such as concrete admit the heat coming in contact with its surface, conduct it inwardly and in effect store it until the surface temperature drops, at which time the heat begins to migrate towards the cooling surface. In this way the heat moves in a wave-like motion as the temperature of its surface changes, alternately storing and emitting heat. It is this property that prompts the idea that thermal mass is not unlike a flywheel in its action, absorbing energy intermittently and emitting it in a more steady flow. The admission of heat into the mass depends upon the nature of the surface, both the colour and the conductivity playing an important part. The darker the colour the better is the ability to absorb radiant heat from the sun, typical factors are 0.9 for black or dark blue compared with 0.2 for white. Care must be taken if the mass is a composite of dissimilar materials, especially if the surface material has a low conductivity. For example, the bare surface of a mass of concrete would have its ability to admit heat halved if it was to be covered with a light carpet.

Thermal mass is an essential component of any passive solar design; it is the system's heat store. 'The aim of storage is to retain the heat collected which is surplus to current needs in order to use it later, when required' (Goulding, 1992, p. 57). However, some exponents of the design of passive solar systems point out that the thickness of a storage wall is no more important than the surface area exposed to the sun. Mazria, for example, suggests that 'an increase in masonry thickness beyond 4 inches (100 mm) results in little change in system performance' (Mazria, 1979, p. 139).

Any passive system must be designed so that it works in a symbiotic relationship with the installed heating system; if the two get out of phase heat will be wasted. The installed system must have a fast response to changing conditions and have an effective thermostatic control. We will return to this subject later.

BRINGING IT ALL TOGETHER

At this stage we now have the means of assessing the possibilities of the natural building heuristic.

Gathering together information about the site climate, making some informed guesses about the pattern of air movement over it and knowing where there will be sunshine and shade, we may make a start on testing some ideas about the form the building may take. It is possible that the need to study the topography may have even prompted an idea for an appropriate form, as indeed did the subject of Rowe's Case Study 2, where the early concept of the design was prompted by a perceived relationship between a new health facility, 'clean living' and a special place by a lake (Rowe, 1991, p. 13).

While recognizing the limits to the application of Givoni's Bioclimatic Chart (its use is illustrated in Fig. 2.5), it is possible to use it to draw up an environmental control strategy. But we need to remember what the chart is telling us. It is in effect saying 'in a given region if the climate is the only determinant, then human comfort may be achieved by either the way the building is designed or, failing that, by installing certain control systems'. However, quite often the climate is not the only determinant and the only possible cause of discomfort. The activity of the occupants, and the machines they use, may be a contributory factor, and Givoni's chart makes no allowance for it. So it may be necessary to review the strategy in the light of information about the way the building is used.

There are other reasons why the strategy may have to be rejected in part or even in whole. Planning the necessary accommodation may show that a shallow plan that enables natural ventilation, is impracticable, or there may be found to be more attractive ways of constructing the building etc., etc. But a start on the next phase has been made and we have moved from dithering over a blank sheet of paper to something that is gathering its form about it; what's more it is ours – well, yours in point of fact.

Bringing together the design determinants of daylighting and natural ventilation can prompt some exciting shapes for a building. We have identified some limitations to adopting a policy of designing for daylight and natural ventilation, but even these constraints should now help you in the search for an appropriate shape to the building. Considering the rules of thumb in a negative way

only, then a desire to daylight and naturally ventilate a building means that it will most probably be a long narrow thing, limited in overall depth to 12 to 14 metres and not at all exciting, but this need not be so. There are now many innovative designs which provide good daylit spaces and acceptable natural ventilation without being limited to a rectangular plan and, as you will see once more, the problems and constraints have prompted (or even allowed) the designers to explore an entirely different architectural form.

We started this chapter looking at the link between a respect for climate and the energy efficient building, whether they are called 'natural' or 'bioclimatic' is not the issue, and have seen that a shape for such a building is prompted by the limitations to the utilization of the natural elements of the site climate. However, there are many building functions which demand a greater depth of plan than that which can be served by natural forces, or it could be that the external climate is not suited to human comfort and best kept outside. For example, although there is a case for designing auditoria so that daylight may be admitted, the times when daylight must be excluded will greatly outnumber those when it is, and the same goes for natural ventilation; at such times mechanical ventilation will be necessary, if not full air-conditioning. In other buildings the heat emitted by the machines which are essential to their function will be such that the rate of ventilation provided by natural means will not be able to cope. It is a fact of commercial life that some owners and tenants see the air-conditioned building as an absolute necessity and will not accept the 'natural building' under any circumstances.

There is also the architectural style which results in a need for air-conditioning, the International Style being a case in point. Therefore there will, to some extent, continue to be a certain reliance on mechanical and electrical systems, from the simple hot water heating installation to the full-blown air-conditioning system. With careful design and thoughtful integration of both building and systems it is, nevertheless, still possible to limit the demand made upon our natural resources and produce exciting buildings.

CHAPTER THREE

DESIGN DEVELOPMENT

ORGANIZING SPACE

Space – the final frontier . . .
Gene Roddenberry (*Star Trek*, 1966)

Space planning is next on our agenda, but don't be fooled by the introductory quotation; this chapter is in no way final, we have some way to go yet.

So far we have looked at ways in which to get started and recognized that the methodology may change to suit a particular type of problem. The first thoughts about a possible solution may be prompted by the shape of the land, or the climate, or a desire to conserve resources. It may come from a desire to follow an architectural style or a designer hero; the list can go on and on. These shadowy ideas will be tested in various ways against the design brief; and the brief itself will be examined in the light of the design concept, for it too develops and is refined during the strategic stages of design. This on-going development of the brief is part of the process of re-structuring the problem, or if you prefer it – defining it, which we met in the first chapter. Eventually the idea begins to acquire shape and form, but it needs to be considered against the size and shape of the area available on the site and matched with the space needed to accommodate the occupants and their activities. Matching the space available to that required for the building is not easy and, above all else, calls for an understanding of how the building is to be used.

Space planning is not just about allocating sufficient space. From a purely functional point of view it is also about placing each separate room in the most effective position relative to the other rooms and to the site, together with ensuring an efficient connection between them. Careful planning will also reduce the need for complex environmental control systems, keeping their operating costs down and reducing the demand for space for their accommodation.

BUBBLE DIAGRAMS

Planning usually starts by graphically exploring the relationships of the site and its climate, access to the building and the functions of the various spaces, and this can be done with the help of a series of 'bubble diagrams'. These are unscaled interaction diagrams which are used in an attempt to resolve these relationships and to explore the possible connections between the various spaces. It is possible to start anywhere making these diagrams, but when you begin to sketch them in you need to envisage how the rooms are used and how the activities may react one upon the other, most certainly keeping noisy activities away from quiet ones. You will find that these diagrams are yet another way of ordering the problem and may only need to be used at the outset of the process; however, their use can be extended, as explained by Edward White in his book *Space Adjacency Analysis* (1986). The process of planning the internal spaces is iterative, and has even been described as an 'exhaustive enumeration' procedure (Stevens, 1990, p. 311). Eventually though, successive variations will produce a pattern that will begin to suggest the shape of a floor plan.

At this stage, when the shape of the building and the pattern of the arrangement of the rooms within it are beginning to emerge, it is not too early to begin to plan the integration of the building with that of the environmental control systems and the utility services. Beginning the process now will save a lot of back-tracking later, when the design will have firmed up to a point where you will not want to modify it to any great extent and perhaps have to let go of some of those beautiful ideas. When designing larger buildings bear in mind the examples of Lloyd Wright and Kahn and that there is an opportunity to make the provision of space for these systems a part of the architectural statement and not a botched afterthought which could damage your building.

All the information needed to make final decisions about the types of environmental control systems that will be required may not be available at such an early stage in the design process, but there should be sufficient data in the brief and knowledge of the site to help you decide whether the various spaces should be heated and ventilated in a simple way or not. This information in the brief will, at the very least, describe the function of the building and the activities going on within it. Therefore, by inference, the environmental conditions that will be needed in the various rooms should be known, together with when those conditions will be needed and for how long. If this data is not given, or it is too tentative, then library research is needed to establish more detailed and specific information and the data placed on record. One way of recording this information is to incorporate it into a Performance Specification.

In effect the Performance Specification describes a space, a room within the building, in terms of the environmental conditions which need to prevail within it. These conditions may be those required or recommended by Acts of Parliament, statutory bodies, professional institutions such as the Chartered Institute of Building Services Engineers, manufacturers, etc. Although the criteria are in the main related to maintaining the health and welfare of the occupants of the building, it is as well to realize that in some instances this has more to do with the quality of the product than the building's function. In this respect it is a sobering thought to realize that the invention and development of the air-conditioning system was prompted by the need to ensure the quality of the goods being manufactured in the textiles and tobacco factories, the comfort of those employed in such places being thought of as necessary, but of secondary importance to the product of their industry.

It is also essential to know when the spaces are to be used and for how long; therefore, in addition to the required environmental conditions there should also be recorded information about the pattern of occupation. Fig. 3.1 shows a typical Performance Specification; its layout would need to be more detailed and specific for complex spaces that require specially controlled conditions, sophisticated servicing systems or where acoustic conditions are special.

Fully developed, the specification is a useful design tool, in that it goes further than simply itemizing the environmental conditions, and contains information about how the room is used and when, which will help to identify similar zones of need, as will be explained later. It can also give the required floor area and volume and, as the process proceeds, an idea of shape and its relationship to the outside. In some ways then, it may actually be regarded as being the entity of the room it describes. There is, as a result of this exercise, more knowledge about the attributes of the rooms which are a component part of the nature of the building being designed. And the performance specification informs the bubble diagram so that it can be developed further in order to assist in the making of subsequent decisions about the environmental control systems, as will be explained shortly.

Although the bubble diagrams cannot be relied on to produce the shape of the building, they will stimulate ideas about a possible form, and this we will explore briefly in the next section. You may, of course, be fortunate and be able to see the shape of the building in your mind's eye without these graphical aids, but if you do not, this does not mean that you will never be a designer, just that you are like the rest of us and it will take a little longer.

Performance Specification for:

Room Reference	Floor Area Volume

Pattern of Occupation	Occupants Age range M or F

Thermal Environment

Temperature during	Internal Heat Gain
Winter	Lighting
Summer	People
(NB unless air conditioned these can not be equal)	Machines
Air Infiltration Rate	
Method of Ventilation: Natural Mechanical	

Visual Environment

Average Daylight Factor	Standard Service Illuminance
Position of Measurement	Type of Lamp

Acoustic Environment	Room Details
NR/NC Curve	Approximate Shape
Room Index	
Noise Source	
Utility Services Special Needs	
	Orientation

FIGURE 3.1 PERFORMANCE SPECIFICATION

FROM BUBBLE DIAGRAMS TO SERVICED ZONES

We have so far seen that bubble diagrams can be used to plan the layout of rooms in a simple building. Let us now go on to look at how they may be used to make early decisions about the allocation of space for the larger components of environmental control systems and to determine the routes of the services distribution network.

For this purpose it is assumed that a special medical unit is to be designed and that the activities within it fall into two main groups. These are typical of such units and comprise a day-care group and a residential, short-stay group. Other buildings are to be placed on the site at some later date, and for this reason, and also because it is desired to keep the building's footprint as small as possible, we are to design a two-storey building, but we may assume

that our unit is to be independent and have its own boilers etc. (This example is loosely based on an actual design and I am indebted to the Oxford Architects Practice for the information and in particular to Jill Grain for her patience).

The first set of diagrams, Fig. 3.2, show which rooms need to be adjacent to each other and the connections between the various rooms in both groups. These requirements will have been arrived at after consulting with the client and, for the sake of brevity, the earlier attempts at drawing the diagrams have not been included. There would have been a great deal of shuffling of the bubbles and their links with each other, and what you see here is a much cleaned up diagram. The linkages are indicated in their level of importance. A few bubbles are indicated as being linked exclusively to other larger ones, and there are also some secondary-level connections, but in the main the strongest links go through a common space. These common spaces,

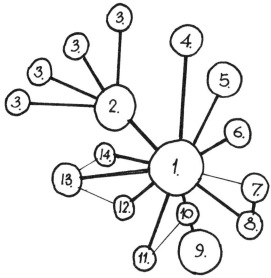
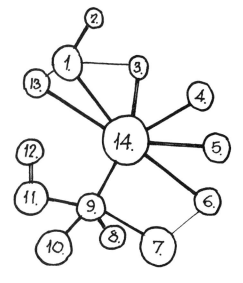

Ground Floor:

1 Entrance, Reception and Waiting	8 Allergy Clinic
2 Consultants	9 Minor Operations
3 Examination Rooms	10 Sub-waiting
4 Pharmacy	11 Sister
5 Administration	12 Clean Utility
6 Photography Suite	13 Treatment
7 Clinical Experiments	14 Dirty Utility

First Floor:

1 Doctors' Offices	8 UV Treatment
2 Treatment	9 Waiting
3 Sister	10 Research/Consultant
4 Day Room	11 Administration
5 Baths	12 Staff Room
6 Kitchen	13 Registrar
7 Conference	14 Central Lobby

FIGURE 3.2 MEDICAL UNIT, BUBBLE DIAGRAMS

or hubs, are obviously an important part of the circulation system and prompt the idea that the plan may radiate from them and that it will be fairly compact if site conditions allow. Fig. 3.3 shows two possible plan forms.

Bear in mind that in some other situation it might have been found that there was little or no need for connections within the group, or perhaps that there was a definite need to separate the component spaces for reasons of noise or cross-infection. In that case the layout would more likely be loose, disconnected and spread out.

Having worked through a series of iterative steps and decided on the best relationship diagram, it can be further developed to help to make those early decisions about the environmental control systems. To do this we need first to construct a zoning diagram based on the bubble diagram. The zones are spatial entities and may be thought of as being made up of rooms which are in the same family. Buffer zones are an example of this. The zones can be determined with regard to the site climate and also to minimize the effect of intrusive noise. We can also make up zones of rooms which need to have similar environmental conditions maintained within them, because the activity of the occupants is similar. There will be others which, while having the same need, will be occupied at different times and

will, therefore, need to have a different response from the environment control system.

It follows that, with some possible exceptions, these zones of similar need may have that need satisfied by the same type of environmental control system, even though it may not be in action at the same time. Typical of the exceptions to this logic are those rooms in which the activity calls for more special treatment, or where heat or foul and toxic gases are being given off by some process and need to be removed. Some rearrangement of the bubble diagram may be found to be necessary as this sorting process is carried out, for there are advantages in having rooms which have similar servicing requirements grouped together; these principally have to do with keeping the services distribution system as small and efficient as possible.

We can now return to the bubble diagram for our hospital unit and draw up the zones. To keep things fairly simple it is assumed that our unit does not treat infectious diseases, nor is it likely to allow the escape of life-threatening radiation or hazards other than those we all face in our normal day-to-day life. Most of the rooms will simply need to be kept at those conditions generally regarded as being comfortable and, with some few exceptions, there is little going on in them that will produce too much

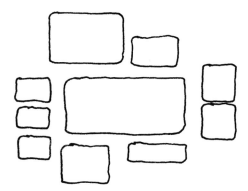
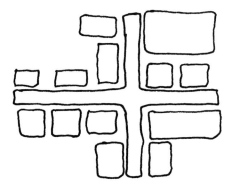

FIGURE 3.3 POSSIBLE PLAN FORMS

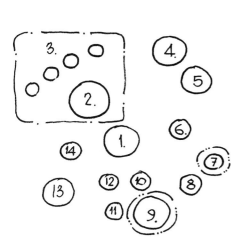
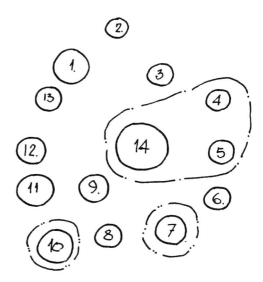

FIGURE 3.4 BUBBLE DIAGRAM, ZONES

heat or noise. In other words, in many of them the environmental conditions will be similar to those experienced in a good standard doctor's office. The exceptions are:

- The Minor Operations Suite, where temperature and humidity need to be controlled.
- Photography, the darkroom of which may need mechanical ventilation.
- Clinical experiments. Here there is a heat source capable of producing conditions which will be very uncomfortable and a possible threat to the success of the experiments.
- UV Treatment, where the equipment also produces heat.
- It may also be necessary to cool the Library/ Conference Room.

With the exceptions itemized above in mind, it is possible to identify two obvious major zones, one being comprised of the rooms serving the Day Care Facility and the other those for the residential patients. However, note that although the consultants' rooms are to have the same environmental conditions as the rest of their 'family', the pattern of occupation will be different. This is because, with the changes presently taking place in the organization of the National Health Service, it is envisaged that the consultants may in the future offer an out-of-hours service and, therefore, their rooms should be regarded as a sub-zone. Going back to the bubble diagrams then, it is possible to outline these zones and also to indicate those rooms which have been identified as having some special need, Fig. 3.4. At the beginning of this exercise I said that the bubble diagrams could not be relied on to produce shape to the building and that they are simply design tools that help to get the internal planning right. They may also prompt some ideas about where to go next. Perhaps the typical hub arrangement or the radiating fingers of the plan may suit the site. The process must also include the selection of suitable environmental control systems, together with the allocation of space for such systems, and the aim of the following chapters is to help you to do that.

And that is where I am going to leave the hospital unit. You may like to carry it along as you read the book and come up with your own final design.

CHAPTER FOUR

SYSTEMS AND INTERCONNECTIONS

MAKING THE LINK

We left the example of the hospital unit at a point where we had developed an outline of the performance needed for the environmental control systems, and had some provisional idea of where the main items of the heating system would be located. This would need to be firmed up later on in the process and more detail would be added as the overall design developed. Just for now, however, we will leave the unit and look at the systems themselves, and the physical links between them, beginning with an examination of the various reasons why certain types of systems are needed. However, we will continue thinking of the components of the systems as 'black boxes' for a while, and only look at them more closely when it becomes necessary. Should you want to dash ahead you may do so, but what follows helps to explain the subsequent chapters.

SYSTEMS AND THE REASONS FOR CHOOSING THEM

In the second chapter we reviewed the principles of daylighting design, natural ventilation and passive solar methods, and saw how they may be applied to the design of the so-called natural building. Following on from there you should, by now, also realize that although the design methodology of the natural building is right for the times we are in, it does not always suit every problem of the built environment, for there are limitations to its overall use. So, although the occupants of the natural building, or its equivalent, may find that natural ventilation and a simple heating system provide acceptable conditions, there are many situations where something more complex will be needed. We will consider some of these situations and the more complex response to them in the form of various environmental control systems. These are depicted in Fig. 4.1 (it is only fair to say that this diagram does not include all the possible systems; it is a generic outline and not a list of the many variations produced by manufacturers).

The diagram is in the form of an algorithm and starts by asking the question 'Is natural ventilation and heating suitable (for the purpose)?' and then proceeds by giving several reasons in an abbreviated form why it may not be so. By now you should be able to reason why there should be these exceptions. However, should you have any doubts about the itemized list that follows refer back to Chapter Two for a more detailed explanation. An explanation of the environmental control systems, the various titles of which are shown below, will develop as we go through the successive chapters.

- Plan form: this indicates that it is not possible to ensure acceptable ventilation by natural means because the plan is too deep, and that top openings cannot be provided to supplement those on the face of the building.

- Site conditions: although it may be possible to

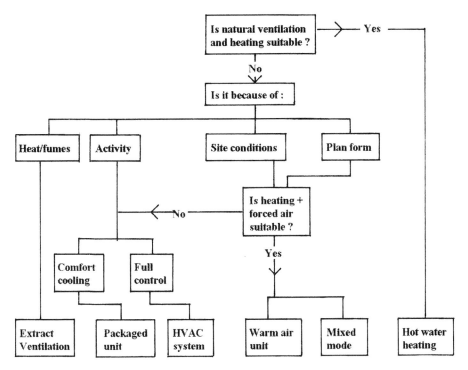

FIGURE 4.1 SYSTEM CHOICE: DETERMINANTS

naturally ventilate the building, the site climate and its condition make it undesirable. This exclusion may be the result of an aggressive natural climate, one that is, for example, hot and dry, or the polluted condition of the site.

● Function/activity: a process within the building may call for controlled clean conditions, or the activity required of the occupants may be such that their health (and efficiency) may be threatened unless the condition of the environment is controlled. There are many activities connected with medicine which demand such conditions, as well as several industrial processes. A need for security against industrial espionage, terrorist action or simple robbery may also prompt the need for a sealed building and locked windows.

● Heat emission: this follows on from the previous case, although in addition there may be a situation where the heat emission needs to be controlled for reasons other than that of the health and welfare of the building's occupants. The centralized computer suite is a typical example, the machines producing the heat and that heat needing to be controlled if they are to work efficiently. It is also just possible that the building design may in itself be the cause; remember that natural ventilation can only cope with so much excess gain from glazing.

No mention has been made of the reasons given by property developers, who in general demand air-conditioning so that their buildings may have perceived prestige and a higher rent value. The desire for a prestigious image in the shape of a fully air-conditioned headquarters office may be another reason, and something similar is also reflected in the price charged for the controlled comfort provided by the upper classes of the hotel trade. However, in the future these 'reasons' may not prove to be sufficient to obtain a waiver from the new draft requirements of the Building Regulations which aim to reduce the unwarranted use of air-conditioning.

With the exception of some industrial applications, the systems which are indicated in the diagram will all need a means of generating heat, and some will require, in addition, a generator of coldness (for want of a better word; 'coolth' has been suggested as being the opposite of warmth, but it has not found favour and, to quote *Webster's Dictionary*, is 'now chiefly a humorous usage'). Heat is normally generated in a boiler or a furnace by burning one of the fuels (although it is also possible to provide it by various other means such as solar panels), and the refrigeration cycle provides the means of cooling. These are the orthodox methods, and for this reason alone we will start with them; later on there will be an explanation of other systems.

THE GENERATION OF HEAT

With a few exceptions, in most central heating installations a fuel is converted into heat in some central plant and that heat is carried around the system by a heat transfer medium, being finally emitted into the room to be heated through a terminal unit. That somewhat bald summary over-looks a whole wealth of possible complexities: in many cases the heat will pass from one transfer medium to another, moving into a different type of environmental control system as it does so. Fig. 4.2 illustrates a typical system, heat first being gener-ated in a boiler and then passing on to two different systems, one being a simple heating system with radiators and the other a system that uses warm air to fulfil its function.

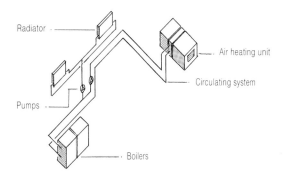

Radiator

Air heating unit

Circulating system

Pumps

Boilers

FIGURE 4.2 DIAGRAMMATIC REPRESENTATION OF A HOT WATER HEATING SYSTEM

HEAT TRANSFER MEDIA

In most installations the heat transfer medium will be one of steam, water or air, the choice being determined by the medium's heat carrying capacity, its suitability to the application, safety and cost. Few buildings now rely on steam as a heat carrying medium. However, it still finds use in some industrial processes, and the generation of electrical power does involve its use, but in the main the heating systems in buildings will have hot water or air circulating through their various heating units.

Water is much cheaper in both capital and operating costs than steam, and the equipment needed to raise its temperature for use as a heating medium is less complex and, properly maintained, not as dangerous in use. In general, water will be pumped through the distribution network of what is described as a 'low temperature' system at about 75 degrees C and at, or a little above, atmospheric pressure. However, as an additional safeguard against accidental burning in nursing homes and public places where there are small children at play, such as a creche, a lower temperature may be chosen for the sake of safety.

Such low temperature hot water systems account for about 90% of the total installations and the present trend is to have them served from boilers that are located close to the zone that is to be heated, rather than have long distribution mains with high capital and running costs. However, in the centralized systems of a large complex of buildings, such as a hospital where the distribution mains are long, these costs can be reduced by circulating the hot water medium at higher temperatures. The higher temperatures make it possible to carry a greater quantity of heat in smaller diameter pipes. For, in that the specific heat of water is 4.187 kJ/kg K, it follows that a given mass of water will absorb and be capable of carrying more heat as its temperature is increased, and the higher tempera-ture water will have a greater heat carrying capa-city. Circulating water temperatures in the range 175 to 250 degrees C are usual in such systems, and to prevent the water from boiling it is pressurized above atmospheric pressure. Obviously there are similar risks to those when using steam, and before the water reaches any heating unit which is in an occupied space both temperature and pressure must be reduced to a safer figure.

Air is even cheaper to obtain than water, clean air may be another matter though, although its heat carrying capacity is far lower. By comparison with water, air is nowhere near as efficient as a heating medium, either as a carrier of heat or in its ability to transfer heat. As an example of the former: a heating load of say 100 kW could be met by warm air moving at 5 m/s in a rectangular duct measuring 1 m by 0.5 m, but by low temperature hot water being carried in a pipe having an internal diameter of 0.063 m. This, as we will see later, is a great disadvantage when space is in high demand, for the ducts carrying the air can be both large and unwieldy (perhaps you now begin to see why both Lloyd Wright and Kahn had to find ways in which to cope with them). Air does have the great advantage, though, that not only can it supply heat, it may also provide the air needed for ventilation and, unlike water, there is no risk of burst pipes under freezing conditions, or of it scalding people either.

BOILERS AND FURNACES

Although the word 'boiler' is in everyday use and familiar to most people, it is in point of fact a misnomer, unless, of course, it refers to a unit which is intended to generate steam. This is because, with some exceptions, most boilers are designed to heat water to a temperature below boiling point and not produce steam. In essence a boiler heating hot water is a simple piece of equipment, it has only a few principal components that need bother us; it is the method of its control that may be somewhat complex.

Fig. 4.3 is a diagram of a typical boiler showing the most basic components.

Some of the heat produced by the boiler escapes to atmosphere because the flue gases are both hot, at about 250 degrees C, and moist. Careful control of the proportion of fuel to the air needed for combustion and the efficient transfer of the heat produced will reduce that loss, but until the early 1980s the design of boilers had not aimed to utilize the latent heat which is present in the moist waste gases. Boilers which are capable of doing this are called 'condensing boilers'. They have an addi-

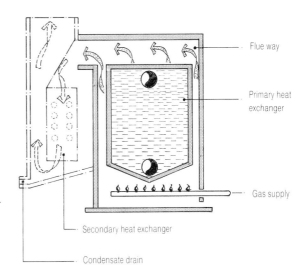

Flue way

Primary heat exchanger

Gas supply

Secondary heat exchanger

Condensate drain

FIGURE 4.3 SIMPLIFIED DIAGRAM OF A GAS FIRED BOILER PLUS SECONDARY HEAT EXCHANGER FOR CONDENSING VERSION

tional, or sometimes an enlarged, secondary heat exchanger that is designed to extract the latent heat from the flue gases. Fig. 4.3 shows the addition of this to the conventional model.

Cooling the gas in this way, so as to utilize the latent heat, causes it to condense (hence the name given to the boiler) and it is for this reason that the materials used for the chimney must be chosen with care and that a drain should be provided for the condensate (CIBSE, 1989). Condensing boilers have operating efficiencies in the range 90 to 95% compared with those of the orthodox in the range 70 to 80%, Fig. 4.4. It is claimed that, over a full heating season, boilers such as these should burn at least 15% less gas than their counterparts the traditional boilers, and that payback of their additional cost is commonly achieved (Department of Energy, 1990).

However, good as it is, the condensing boiler is not suited to all buildings. A study by The Building Services Research and Information Association showed that they are particularly suitable for use in buildings which have long periods of operation and that one used in isolation is rarely economic (BSRIA, 1990). Where two boilers are installed only one may be the condensing model, and it will be used as the 'lead' boiler; that is, it will be called on first so that it is

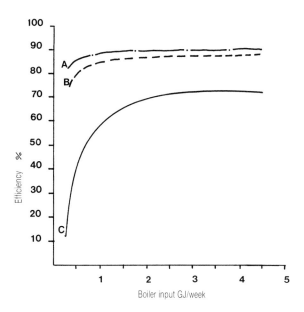

A: radiators oversized 100%
B: radiators of usual size
C: efficiency of a traditional boiler

FIGURE 4.4 OPERATING EFFICIENCY OF A
CONDENSING BOILER (FROM DEPARTMENT OF ENERGY
BEST PROGRAMME 1992)

more often fully loaded.

All boilers should be sited with care. Those used for buildings other than those of domestic scale will produce noise to some extent, so do not place them close to a noise-sensitive zone, and remember that they need air for combustion, a means of discharging the flue gases safely to atmosphere, and access for maintenance and possible removal if there is a need to replace them. Fig. 4.5 summarizes these requirements and shows a typical layout.

The heat output required from a boiler installation depends upon

● the rate at which heat is lost through the fabric of the building, plus that lost by the infiltration of air and ventilation,

● the quantity of hot water that is needed for domestic use, such as washing, or for a process,

● any heat emitted wastefully by the pipes circulating the hot water around the building.

HEAT LOSS

There is insufficient space in this book to explain in any detail the whole subject of heat transfer and the built form; you should refer to the Further Reading List for books that do so. You need to know why it is that the loss of heat through the fabric of a building is a function of the thermal properties of the materials of construction, the exposed surface area of the material and the difference in temperature of the heated space and the outside air.

It is often tempting to think that the contribution of solar gain and the emission of heat from the occupants, plus any being given off by the machines they may use, may be taken to offset the heat loss and therefore reduce that calculated to be required from the boiler. Given some thought, however, it will be realized that the boilers need to be warming the building prior to occupation and before there is any internal heat gain. These gains are taken into account when the annual consumption of energy is calculated.

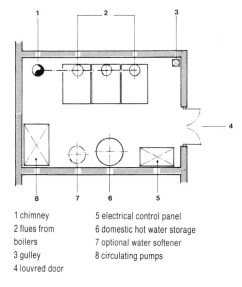

1 chimney
2 flues from boilers
3 gulley
4 louvred door
5 electrical control panel
6 domestic hot water storage
7 optional water softener
8 circulating pumps

FIGURE 4.5 OUTLINE REQUIREMENTS OF A
BOILER HOUSE

ALLOCATION OF SPACE FOR BOILER PLANT

Fig. 4.6 gives an indication of the space needed for boilers and their ancillaries such as pumps and thermal controls; this is indicated as a function of

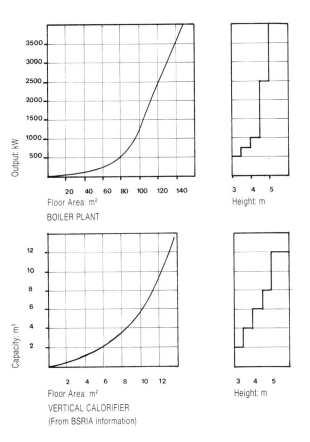

FIGURE 4.6 SPACE ALLOCATION FOR BOILER PLANT

the heat output of the equipment and therefore you will need to know how to make an approximate assessment of this. There is little point in being too accurate at this stage in the design process, so content yourself with an assessment rather than a detailed calculation. There are various ways of doing this.

The easiest way is to adopt a rule of thumb, bearing in mind that these do have limits to their application. They will tell you nothing about the thermal efficiency of the building, whether it is designed to utilize solar gain or anything of that nature, and therefore the information they provide must be open to question and will need to be verified later in the design process.

Building Type	Maximum Heat Requirement (W/m³)
Offices	15 to 25
Factories, small	20 to 25
large	20

Later, when the building is nearing the final design stage and you have a good idea of what it will be constructed from, the accuracy of the assessment can be improved by making a calculation based on a typical module of the building. Calculate the heat loss for the module and by dividing the result by the volume of the space you have an improved rule of thumb that you can apply to the total volume.

REFRIGERATION, THE GENERATION OF A COOLING EFFECT

The refrigerator, or as it was known originally, 'the freezing machine', was the invention of an American medical doctor, John Gorrie. He was prompted to find a way of making ice during the summer months in an effort to help his patients who had malaria. He took out a patent for his machine in May 1851, but never found a financial backer for it and died before it found a use (Burke, 1978).

Although few homes in the UK are air-conditioned, most now have a refrigerator in the kitchen and it works more or less on the same principle as the larger commercial units. It too depends upon the thermo-dynamic properties of certain heat transfer media and how they may be manipulated. We will cover heat pumps shortly, but it is worth mentioning at this point that they operate in the same way, they just have some additional valves.

The explanation of the refrigeration cycle is fairly simple, but somewhat perversely I am going to start by talking about steam. In the previous section we covered the use of steam and water, and mention was made of the fact that water could be heated above its boiling point without boiling occurring if its pressure was increased to above that of the atmosphere. The reverse is also true. As an example of this fact: at the top of Mount Everest the atmospheric pressure is said to be 37 kPa (at sea level it is about 101 kPa) and water can be made to boil at that pressure at a temperature of 75 degrees C (you may like to know that, arising from this situation, it is not possible to make a good cup of tea on top of Mount Everest). When water boils we know that evaporation takes place as its state changes from that of a liquid to that of a gaseous vapour.

You must also know that if you wet your finger and then blow on it long enough it will become dry again. The moisture having been evaporated, the heat required to bring about the change of state came from your finger, and you know that because your finger became cooler.

This process of evaporating a liquid can therefore be seen as a cooling process (technically it is known as an 'adiabatic process'), and refrigeration is accomplished by similarly evaporating a liquid heat exchange medium, but in a closed cycle.

REFRIGERATION SYSTEMS: THE VAPOUR COMPRESSION CYCLE

The medium used in this system, known as a refrigerant for obvious reasons, is chosen because it will vaporize at atmospheric pressure and normal temperature and also suffer a reversal of its state and condense back to a liquid when cooled by air or water that is at normal temperature, but with a pressure well above that of the atmosphere. A typical refrigerant will, at a pressure of 300 kPa, have a boiling point of 0 degrees C, but at a pressure of 1000 kPa the boiling point will be 40 degrees C.

Fig. 4.7 shows a simplified line diagram of a vapour compression cycle refrigerator. In the cyclical process which goes on in this system, the refrigerant is circulated by an electric compressor and it goes through a cycle of alternate compression, liquefaction, expansion and evaporation. This is known as the 'vapour compression cycle' and it is the basis of the majority of refrigeration units.

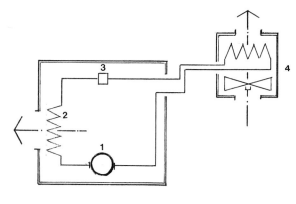

1 compressor/circulating pump
2 condenser, heat rejection
3 expansion valve
4 cooling coil (evaporator) fan powered

FIGURE 4.8 DIRECT EXPANSION REFRIGERATION SYSTEM

A unit such as this may be used within an air-conditioning system in one or two ways. It may, for example, have the evaporator directly in the path of the air mass which is to be cooled so that it would absorb heat as the air passed through it, Fig. 4.8. A unit such as this is referred to as a 'direct expansion system', or by the abbreviation DX. Alternately, the refrigerating unit may first chill water, which in turn is circulated through a heat exchanger over which passes the air to be cooled, Fig. 4.9. There are advantages and disadvantages to both methods and these we will touch upon later when we come to air-conditioning systems.

Whichever system is used they will need a means whereby the heat which is to be transferred from the refrigerant in the condenser is either dumped or utilized elsewhere. It was, until the need for energy conservation became important, normal practice to discharge the heat taken from the condenser to atmosphere, and this as done through a component commonly called a cooling tower. It is now more usual either to use that heat to provide hot water for washing, or to circulate it through a heating system, or to store it for use later. Despite these economic practices it is still necessary to have some means of dumping the heat should it become surplus to requirements, and a cooling tower will therefore still be needed.

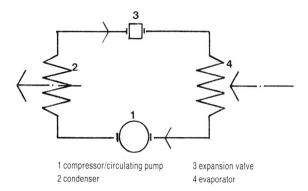

1 compressor/circulating pump   3 expansion valve
2 condenser   4 evaporator

FIGURE 4.7 VAPOUR COMPRESSION REFRIGERATION CYCLE

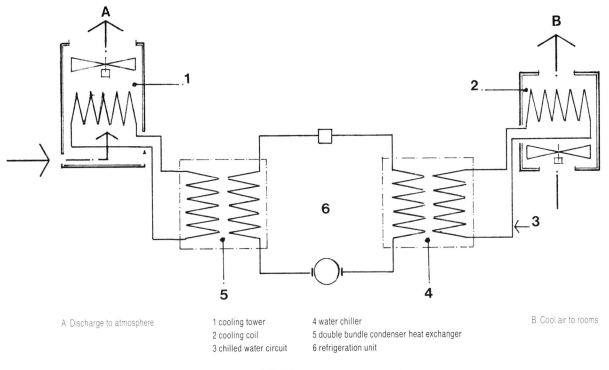

A Discharge to atmosphere

1 cooling tower
2 cooling coil
3 chilled water circuit

4 water chiller
5 double bundle condenser heat exchanger
6 refrigeration unit

B Cool air to rooms

FIGURE 4.9 WATER CHILLER UNIT

The name 'cooling tower' can conjure up a vision of the towers seen around power stations; however, the units we are presently discussing may be big, but they are not that big. They do have similar functions, in that ambient air is used to provide the cooling effect, and therefore they must have a free flow of air moving through them. Like their big brethren they can be seen to emit water vapour, although not as quite the same size clouds. They differ in one important feature in that they produce an intermittent noise and this can be as much as 80 dB. The unit then contains a heat exchanger, through which flows either the refrigerant, which itself is carrying the heat taken from the condenser, or water which circulates through another heat exchanger so as to cool the refrigerant and then carry that heat to the cooling tower. Air is forcibly circulated over the heat exchanger in the unit by a fan, Fig. 4.10.

There are two main types of cooling towers, and the description above has concentrated on only one. The alternative, sometimes known as the economizer condenser, has dropped from favour

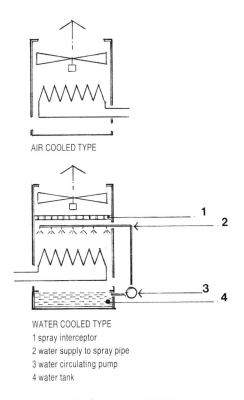

AIR COOLED TYPE

WATER COOLED TYPE
1 spray interceptor
2 water supply to spray pipe
3 water circulating pump
4 water tank

FIGURE 4.10 COOLING TOWER

because it has caused the spread of the Legionnaire bacillus. This type of unit worked on the same principle as the one so far described, but it was made more efficient by spraying water over the heat exchanger. The water enhanced the evaporative cooling effect, but if the unit was not rigorously maintained and kept clean it provided an excellent breeding place for the bacilli, which were carried in the moist air leaving the tower and spread to the neighbouring areas. The space required for the refrigerator unit and the cooling tower can be determined from Fig. 4.11.

THE ABSORPTION CYCLE

In the vapour compression cycle the cooling effect is brought about by evaporating the refrigerant at a low pressure, the reduction being caused by placing the evaporator on the suction side of the compressor. As an alternative to this method the reductive cooling can be brought about by the absorption of the refrigerant in a suitable solvent. Ammonia and even water may be used as a refrigerant, and the absorbing material is often lithium bromide, or silica gel; the latter you may be more familiar with as type of drying agent, and one which may be used to prevent the damage of

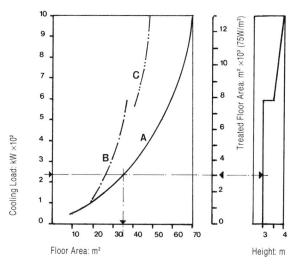

A: Refrigeration plant
B: Single air cooled unit
C: Two air cooled units

FIGURE 4.11 SPACE ALLOCATION FOR REFRIGERATION EQUIPMENT

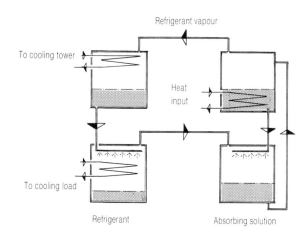

FIGURE 4.12 ABSORPTION REFRIGERATION CYCLE

instruments by damp conditions. If you are familiar with the use of silica gel, then you will know that it has to re-activated from time to time by heating it; the absorption agent in this cycle is treated in a similar way after the cooling action has taken place. If water is the chosen refrigerant it is evaporated, as in the previously described vapour compression cycle, during the heat absorbing phase, and the resulting vapour is then absorbed by a strong concentration of the lithium bromide. This solution of now weak lithium bromide and water is then pumped to a regenerator for reconcentration by heating. The water is then driven off and continues to circulate on to the condenser as a vapour, where it will be cooled before moving into the evaporation phase once again, Fig. 4.12.

The interesting feature of this type of refrigerator is that it does not use a compressor to generate pressure differentials; instead two less powerful pumps are used to move the refrigerant around and to recirculate the absorber. Even more interesting, and seemingly contradictory, is that the absorption cycle uses heat to regenerate the absorber. As a consequence it is less noisy, has a reduced demand for electrical power and is able to utilize any heat which is surplus to the requirements of the environmental control system, a feature which we shall touch on shortly. Its biggest disadvantages are that it operates at a lower efficiency than the vapour compression machine and it is far bulkier.

THE HEAT PUMP

This unit is regarded by some with an awe something akin to that afforded to perpetual motion, and yet it is in reality only a modification to the refrigeration cycle which allows the roles of the condenser and the evaporator to be reversed.

Heat pumps were originally designed to provide both cooling and heating in due season. When the weather was hot you used it as an air-conditioner, providing cool air, and when the season changed and heating became necessary the machine was switched over to become a heater. This was achieved by reversing the flow of the refrigerant through the unit. Fig. 4.13 shows the loop around the compressor and the valves which made it possible.

Heat pumps utilize sources of low-grade heat; in effect they 'pump up' the value of the heat to make it useful. Imagine putting a container of water in the domestic refrigerator in order to make some ice cubes. The evaporator part of the system is usually the freezing compartment at the top of the refrigerator, and it absorbs heat from the water. The heat from the water is circulated around by the refrigerant and is dumped from the condenser section, which is the coil of thin tubes on the outside of the back wall of the refrigerator. In a student house it will have dead spiders and their webs clinging to it, but you will still be able to feel some slight heat coming off it. The heat you feel is the heat which has been taken out of the water to make the ice. Now, instead of a small pan of water imagine a river, any mass of water slightly above freezing, or a waste gas which is to be discharged to atmosphere. If we now bring that into contact with the evaporator of our larger refrigerator set and transfer the heat to the condenser, then we could make use of some of the heat.

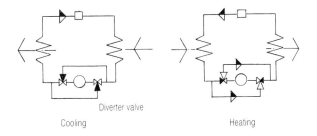

Cooling   Diverter valve   Heating

FIGURE 4.13 HEAT PUMP

I always think of the process in this way. If someone, for some reason or other, decided to change a £1 coin for 100 pennies and then, perhaps because there was a hole in his pocket, scattered the pennies one by one over a fairly large area, very few people would consider them worth the energy to pick them up one by one. If it was possible to use a little energy to somehow collect the 100 coins in a pile, they would then have a collective worth equal to the original and be worth picking up. This, in effect, is what a heat pump does; it makes a scattered, low-energy source valuable. The energy input, represented by collecting and picking up the pile of pennies, is the power which drives the compressor, and the heat pump system recovers the otherwise less than useful heat in the source. We will return to the use of the heat pump later.

TOTAL ENERGY, COMBINED HEAT AND POWER, CO-GENERATION

These titles all refer to the same engineering concept, that of the generation of heat and electrical power by the same unit, and do it in a manner which makes both sources of energy useful. In the UK electrical power was, until privatization, produced in large power stations and circulated around the national grid. This had one big disadvantage, and that was, and still is to a great extent, that the average overall operating efficiencies can be as low as 30%.

This poor performance would not normally be accepted by the engineering profession, but it was the result of a single-mindedness on the part of the power industry. Their remit was to produce a source of reliable power for the nation, and this they did; for it must be admitted that power losses are very rare, and even then are due to either some local fault or industrial strike action. Unfortunately the Central Electricity Generating Board (CEGB) pursued that remit with their blinkers on, thinking only of the production of electricity and considering the heat, which was an inevitable by-product, a nuisance to be rejected.

What was needed was a re-ordering of the problem. The orthodox way to produce electricity, setting aside hydro-power etc., is to raise steam by burning a fossil fuel and have it eventually drive what is, to put it crudely, a dynamo. An alternative way of producing power is by using an internal combustion engine. A motor vehicle has an internal combustion engine that, in addition to its main duty of providing the means of propulsion, not only produces electricity to light the car headlights and charge the battery, but also generates useful heat. On a much larger scale, but in a similar way, the ocean liner, the size of a small city, and complete with its citizens, performs these multi-functions. In a similar way a whole industry, or a building, can be supplied with the electricity produced by an internal combustion engine, or a gas fired turbine, Fig. 4.14, and if the heat is utilized then the overall efficiency can be in the region of 80%.

The idea of generating both heat and electricial power is not new, for the technology was in use during the last century. In fact the first combined heat and power plant, built in Manchester at the turn of the century, is said to be still in use. However, the improvement depends largely on the utilization of the heat that is produced in addition to the electrical power; if it is wasted then the whole operation becomes inefficient. Also, financial viability is not simply a function of making the operation thermally efficient, it requires the greatest use of the investment, and therefore the power unit must be in

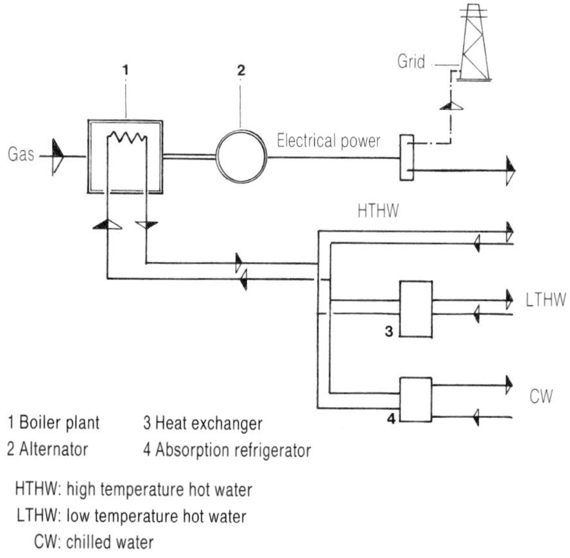

1 Boiler plant   3 Heat exchanger
2 Alternator   4 Absorption refrigerator

HTHW: high temperature hot water
LTHW: low temperature hot water
CW: chilled water

FIGURE 4.14 COMBINED HEAT AND POWER GENERATION

full operation, producing both electricity and heat, and these must find a market.

PATTERNS OF DISTRIBUTION

Having discussed boiler plant and refrigeration we now need to turn our attention to the means of distributing the heat transfer media. The media will be circulated around the building, making the link between either the boiler or the refrigerator and the rooms served by the systems, and it will be carried in pipes and ducts, depending on the medium chosen. I have already urged you to plan for this distribution system and suggested that the construction of zoning diagrams at the strategic stage of design is the best way of doing this. It is advisable to identify where a particular type of environmental control system is needed, to arrange together as many rooms as possible that share that need, and to place the means of satisfying it as close to the zone as is practicable. For, although the allocation of sufficient space for the various services can be a problem, it is often only made worse by the pattern of the distribution.

Every building has within it services other than the environmental control systems, and yet the descriptions you will have read so far have concentrated upon the latter. There are some good reasons for this selective approach, the main one being that if the book attempted to cover all the possible services it would become a monster, an omnibus text book. Such a book would not be in accord with the aim of this one, which is to produce an aid to design that you might want to keep close to hand. Arising from that aim was the need for selection, and the environmental control systems were chosen because:

● Of the total capital cost of all the services they cost the most. Building services can amount to between 30 to 40% of the total capital cost of a building (in a hospital or a special laboratory this can be even higher) and the space heating, air treatment etc. would make up about half of that amount. Care in planning for their accommodation is therefore necessary if this cost is to be kept within acceptable limits.

● With the possible exception of the lifts, the main components of the environmental control system are the largest single item, and therefore their accommodation calls for the most careful planning. In addition, the ducts that carry the conditioned air may have a large cross-sectional area, which means that they are unwieldy and difficult to manipulate when a change of direction is required and, even worse, there are always at least two of them.

Having said that, you must bear in mind that, with the exception of housing and the simplest of other types of buildings, all buildings will have, in addition to the environmental control systems, one or more of the following:

● Utility services such as: drinking water; domestic hot water; drainage, both foul and 'grey', and electrical supplies.
● Telecommunication system.
● Lifts, if multi-storey, especially for those who cannot climb the stairs, and perhaps escalators.
● Fire-fighting facilities: fire hoses, dry risers, sprinkler systems (which will need a large water store), alarms, fireman's lift and, if there is a computer suite, a special fire-fighting installation.
● Computer systems, network distribution and connection through the telecommunication system.
● Building management systems, security installation and public address.
● Catering facilities, kitchen, canteen, drink dispensers etc.

In addition, there may be, in the larger establishments, such a thing as a social centre which provides a swimming pool, squash courts, multi-gym etc.

Many of these have been fully described in several specialist text books, and these are included in the list of Further Reading so that you may become more familiar with them. However, text books always lag behind today's practice; new developments appear regularly and you should refer to the various professional journals and trade magazines in an effort to keep up to date.

ENERGY CENTRES AND PLANT ROOMS

Although the day of the large, central boiler house is passing there are still good reasons for a main plant room, in particular when there is a combined heat and power installation, but also if the building has a compact shape. A Case Study of the Royal Life Offices, Peterborough, is to be found in Chapter Twelve, and it is a successful example of this type of planning.

It has been suggested by the Energy Efficiency Office that the fans and circulating pumps of an air-conditioning system usually need almost twice as much electrical energy as the refrigeration. In an effort to reduce the energy needed to circulate the heating and cooling media around the distribution network, the trend now is therefore towards the decentralization of the main items of the system. Most buildings will, therefore, have more than one room to house the equipment which will generate heat and also provide a means of cooling.

Traditionally boiler plant was placed in the basement, and in the past there were some good reasons why this had been done. In the days before circulating pumps came into more common use there was a need to ensure that the thermo-syphonic action that created the circulation was as powerful as possible. This meant that there had to be a good difference in the height of the heating units and that of the boiler. Putting the boiler in the basement, well below the heating system on the ground floor, thus enhanced the thermo-syphonic effect. There are still some good reasons for keeping the boiler down below, but these are mainly related to the noise that may be produced. Less worthy is the other deciding factor, and that is that there was a left-over space in the basement and nowhere else to put them. However, with proper provision and attention to the attenuation of the noise produced by the equipment, there are few reasons why the boiler should not be on the roof; in fact in tall multi-storey buildings there are often plant rooms at a mid-height position. Also remember that, in general, all boilers need a chimney, and that if the plant is in the basement the chimney must run the whole height of the building and protrude above the roofline.

Refrigerator sets are also producers of noise; in addition they vibrate and this must not be allowed to be conducted through the structure of the building. For this reason they are best placed in the basement, although it is possible to place them anywhere within the building, but they must be isolated from the structure for the reasons given, and also there must be a connection with the cooling tower situated outside, and this should be as direct as possible. Many Local Authorities will not allow the boilers and the refrigerator sets to be housed in the same room because of the risk of fire.

If the building is to be mechanically ventilated there must be a means of driving the conditioned air through the building. We will discuss this in more detail later, and you will need to refer between this section and the later one when you get to it, but for now accept that there could be a unit called an 'air handling unit' and that this would need piped connections to the boiler and perhaps also to the refrigeration set. They are somewhat easier to site, access and noise not being as difficult as the other large components.

Air handling units are usually delivered to site as a number of packages, and therefore access for their installation is not as critical as that for the other main items; the floor area they need, once assembled, can be just as large though. It is possible to specify a limit to the level of noise produced by the unit. This is sometimes referred to as 'plant break-out noise', and the moving parts which could cause vibration can be isolated as part of the package. In that the air handling unit does just that, it handles air, there is a definite need for a supply of clean, outside air to it and a means whereby the vitiated air may be discharged to atmosphere, Fig. 4.15. These connections are best made as direct as possible (see Chapter Four for more detail) and the best place for the unit is on the roof, or if a suitable site can be found for it, outside, but protected from the weather and damage. Fig. 4.16 indicates how much space needs to be allocated for a typical air handling unit; this will vary depending on how the various components are arranged. There are many such arrangements, the most important feature of

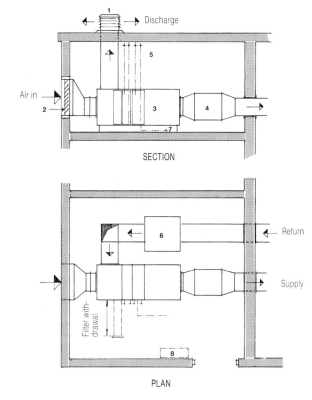

1 weathered outlet for vitiated air
2 louvred air inlet
3 air handling unit
4 noise attenuator (optional)
5 hot and chilled water supply to the unit
6 extract fan
7 drain from cooling coil to gulley
8 electrical control panel

FIGURE 4.15 TYPICAL ACCOMMODATION FOR AN AIR HANDLING UNIT

which is that the flow of air through the unit must make sense and that the two fans are positioned so that they carry out their appropriate function.

Access to all these major items is important, for the purpose of the initial installation and subsequent maintenance. There is a natural law of perversity that dictates that if the access is poor and the equipment is difficult to get at, then there will be a need to remove it in whole or part before too long. More seriously, if there is too little space in the room then it will be difficult to ensure that the installation is done correctly, and if getting to it is less easy than that of other parts of the system, then regular servicing will be neglected. It is also absolutely

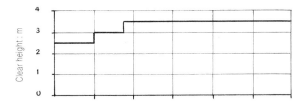

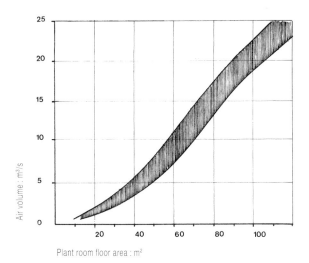

FIGURE 4.16 SPACE ALLOCATION FOR AIR HANDLING UNIT

necessary to think about the means of escape in the case of fire, especially if the room is a long one and the access door is at the far end.

In summary, a plant room needs to be large enough for the equipment it houses and to provide access to it; it also needs to have an efficient shape and not be merely a left-over piece of floor area. It should serve the purpose of the equipment that it is to accommodate and be sensibly positioned with respect to that purpose. It must have means of escape in the case of fire.

HORIZONTAL DISTRIBUTION OF SERVICES

You will have realized that the distribution system may have one or two parts. In a simple heating system there will be just one part and that will be a direct connection between the boiler generating the heat and a heating unit in the room. In the more complex system there is most likely to be a primary circuit that circulates either the heating or cooling medium from the boiler or refrigerator to a sort of go-between. The latter may be a heat exchanger, or it could be what is commonly known as a cooling coil, which could be part of an air handling unit, and this has circulating through it conditioned air – the second part of the distribution system, Fig. 4.17.

As was pointed out in the previous chapter, the horizontal distribution route often follows that of the building's general circulation pattern. Obviously both the chosen route and its position must work with the structural system rather than against it (see Chapter Eight for an explanation of this). It is better to keep the distance travelled short (remember the zoning diagram in Fig. 3.4 and the reasons for it). Long routes, which make connections with several rooms or buildings, will generally require more horizontal space, because the pipes and/or ducts will need to be a larger to carry a greater volume of heat transfer medium. Installation costs and pumping costs will also be higher. Keep cross-overs in the distribution mains to a minimum and, in the case of ducts, avoid them like the plague.

VERTICAL DISTRIBUTION

Spaces for the vertical distribution routes need to be designed in conjunction with the other building elements, the most important of which are the structural elements – the columns, the sheer walls,

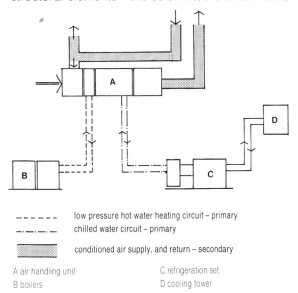

- - - - - - low pressure hot water heating circuit – primary
- · - · - · - chilled water circuit – primary

conditioned air supply, and return – secondary

A air handling unit   C refrigeration set
B boilers   D cooling tower

FIGURE 4.17 PRIMARY & SECONDARY CIRCUITS

and any wind bracing, together with stairways, lift shafts and lift lobbies. Typically these coalesce into core areas, and the vertical route can usefully be part of that common space. However, take care that the route is not cut off from the floor it is intended to serve by the walls of the lift shaft etc. If the services shaft is to contain ducts carrying air then its shape must be sympathetic to the layout of the structural grid. If not then the space required when those ducts change to a horizontal route will need to be deeper (the reason for this and other normative rules will become clearer as we progress into system analysis).

In a multi-storey building the space needed for the vertical core can be large; truly tall buildings such as the 40 to 70-storey sky scrapers in the USA may have cores, which include lifts, their lobbies, stairs, toilets and the services, with an area that represents some 27% of the area of each floor served by the core. However, a generally accepted rule of thumb, for buildings other than the somewhat gross sky scraper, is that the total area of a vertical shaft for services only is about 2% of the

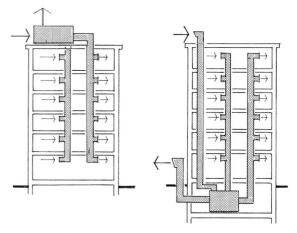

FIGURE 4.18 POSITION OF AIR HANDLING UNIT AND CONNECTIONS TO DUCTS

gross floor area of the building. Care should be taken over the position of the vertical core or services shaft if the best use of space, in the shaft itself and the horizontal service zones, is to result, Fig. 4.18. As a guide to the position, arrange the shaft so that it serves a floor space within a radius of between 15 to 21 metres. The shape, number and

Position & Number of Cores

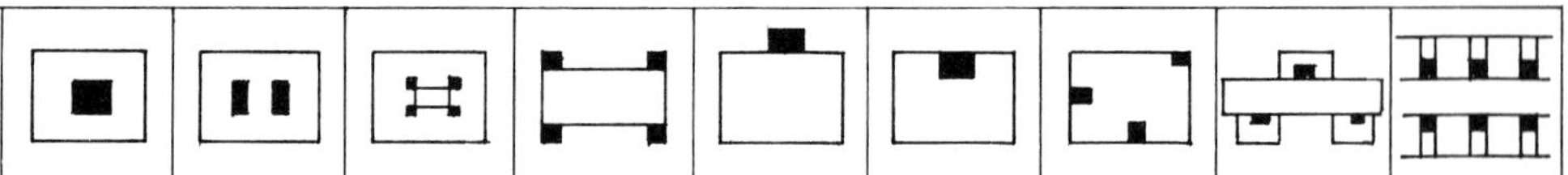

Rentable space	1	2	3	1	1	2	3	3	2
Number of tenants	Large single	Large single	Single/Multi	Single/Multi	Large single	Large single	Multi	Multi	Multi
Flexibility of layout	3	4	1	1	5	4	3	2	5
Example of use			Gateway II	Larkin				Nucles	Hotel
Daylighting & contact	4 2	4 3	1	4 2	5 3	4 3	3	4 2	2
Ease of services connection	1	2	1	1	2–3	3–4	2	1	1
Pumping costs	2	2	1	1	5	4	1	3–4	4
Structural integrity	1	1	2	2	4	4	3	1	1

Information from several sources

FIGURE 4.19 TYPES OF BUILDINGS AND THE POSITION OF SERVICE CORES AND SHAFTS

position of the service cores depends upon the type of building. A high-rise but compact building may need only one, and it is more likely to be in common with the lift shaft, stairs etc.; even so its position is important on several counts, Fig. 4.19.

If the same building is to be occupied by multi-tenants, then the provision of several smaller shafts will make the build-up of leasing more economic and later allow greater flexibility when in use. Alternatively a hotel, a nursing home or a university hall of residence would be better serviced by several shafts to carry the heavy and more frequent demand for the utility services of water, drainage and electricity. All the services in the shafts must be accessible, but because they run through all the floors they can be the cause of the spread of fire, and poorly designed access doors increase that risk. Attention must be paid to this problem and also to horizontal ducts where they pass from one fire compartment to another.

FLOOR AND CEILING SPACES

Until fairly recently the most commonly used space for services running through offices was the ceiling. The suspended ceiling can hide a whole host of pipes, ducts, trailing wires and light fittings, together with badly finished concrete with very little apparent designed planning. It can also be the battle ground of competing trades and result in an unco-ordinated mess where the lights do not integrate with either the air outlets or the modular arrangement of a laid-in tile system.

The impact that IT would have on office design was made clear in the ORBIT (Office Research on Buildings and Information Technology) report based on a study made by the DEGW Group in 1983. With the arrival of the IT office there came a need for additional cables and more air-conditioning apparatus, and the raised floor with a clear height of between 150–200 mm became the norm, Fig. 4.20. There evolved from this new ways of lighting the space with uplighters, of supplying conditioned air and cables directly into the work stations, and furniture that would integrate with the new arrangement (see Chapter Eight).

These service zones place an increasing burden on space requirements, and on the cost of the

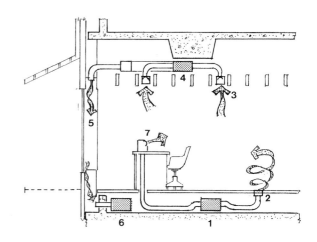

1 supply duct
2 swirl outlet
3 return through luminaire
4 extract duct
5 return air through glazing unit
6 fan coil unit
7 individual air supply

FIGURE 4.20 TYPICAL IT OFFICE

building; saving a few millimetres per floor can in a multi-storey building pay for the construction of an extra floor. Integrating the design of the structure and the services, particularly the air-conditioning system and its air ducts, is therefore very important and we will return to it later in the book.

Since the time of the ORBIT study several coincident events have produced a lowering in the demand for space by the IT office. In a recent article John Worthington of DEWG identifies these events as the move to structured networks of cables, rather than the ever-growing number of cabling systems, the realization that the amount of heat generated by the occupants, the machines and the lighting was not as great as was predicted, and a radical change in office practice and staffing levels (Worthington, 1992). All of which means that the design of such offices is being re-thought. Raised floors will still be in evidence in many prestigious headquarters buildings, but they will be much reduced and there may be a case for using either the ceiling void or the raised floor, but not both.

Exposing the structural slab, by not having a suspended ceiling, carries with it the possibility of utilizing it as thermal mass to reduce fluctuations in the internal temperature (see Chapter Two) and to reduce the need for air-conditioning. This potential may not always be fully realized, however, as was shown by a Department of Energy study of IT offices, if the building is not designed to facilitate night-time cooling of the exposed slab (Evans, 1992).

An alternative to the service zone above the ceiling or below the floor is to put the services on show, what Reyner Banham called 'Exposed Power', the exposed environmental control aesthetic (Banham 1969, p. 234). Not all buildings will lend themselves to the concept, and it is not an easy design option either; it calls for careful integration of all the components of the environmental control system and the interior design. Large components always have the greater possibility of looking sculptural than masses of separate smaller pipes and cables, the standard of workmanship must be high and any insulated surfaces must have an attractive finish. The ultimate in the adoption of the concept is, of course, the design of Centre Nationale d'Art et de Culture Georges Pompidou, Paris. It is perhaps more engineering than architecture with its dramatically stated structure and large external ducts painted in frank, primary colours. More recently, but smoother and city sophisticated, is the Lloyd's Building in London.

As has been said a number of times in this book, designing space for services need not be a chore and the equipment dismissed to the basement or hidden behind a wall like an Anchorite nun. It can be part of the design statement and great architects have realized that fact and acted upon it to dramatic effect.

CHAPTER FIVE

HEATING

SYSTEM CHOICE

It is much easier [in making a decision about the best heating method] … to determine what we ought not to do, than to draw final conclusions as to the best course for adoption in each case.

E.R. Robson, Architect (1835–1912)

We have considered the application of natural ventilation and the limits to its effectiveness when applied in certain situations and to the function of some buildings. Where the ventilation can be brought about by natural means then a saving in energy can result, and the building may be heated by fairly simple means. In this chapter we will look at the various methods of heating a building and its occupants.

Before moving on it is worth remembering that the orthodox calculation of the heat output required by the system is based on the heat lost through the fabric of the building and by the infiltration of outside air. Obviously that basis is directly related to providing an acceptable thermal environment for the occupants, but that acceptability does not depend upon the performance of the heating system alone, for it is tied up with the nature of what may be called 'the thermal form' of the building. By this I mean not just the thermal performance of the fabric of the building, both the transparent and the opaque, or the way it is naturally ventilated, but also its shape and even its internal finishes. If you accept this idea then you should realize that designing a heating system involves more than aiming to

provide a certain air temperature within it during the heating season, and that it requires the combined effort of the building design team. The system must be chosen with due regard to this nature of the building, the site climate and the needs of the occupants.

So, although I have so far married the idea of natural ventilation with what has been called a 'simple heating system' (they have been described as such to differentiate them from the other systems which may provide mechanical ventilation as well as heating), choosing an appropriate system may be far from simple.

The discussion so far has concentrated on the central systems, but as you will see later, heat can be supplied by a localized, self-contained piece of equipment. Central systems will, if properly designed and located, be much quieter than the localized unit; they tend to provide a better standard of environmental control and also give longer periods of service. On the other hand, the local unit can be cheaper initially, need less space, be easier to install and maintain and also be better suited to multi-tenanted buildings.

THE CENTRAL DISTRIBUTION SYSTEM

You will have realized from the preceding chapter that hot water is the chosen heat transfer medium for the 'central heating system' and that the water is heated in a boiler, but just in case you skipped over that part let us fill the picture out.

A central, low-pressure hot water heating system has four main components:

● A boiler (which you may now know is a misnomer; see Chapter Four where you will find a description) which will generate heat from, in general, the burning of one of the fossil fuels; although the heat may come from other sources such as a heat pump, solar panels, a co-generation unit and even electricity.

● A distribution network, that will be comprised of a two-pipe system. Through one of these the hot water will flow outward from the boiler to the various heating units, and through the other pipe the cooler water will return back to the boiler to be reheated. In the description of such systems the two pipes are therefore known as the 'flow and return'.

● An electrical pump, or pumps if there is more than one zone, that circulates the hot water around the system.

● Terminal heating units that transfer the heat from the hot water to the room.

There will also be a thermal control system to regulate the output of heat in accordance with the needs of the occupants and the prevailing weather conditions, and also a number of valves that may be used to isolate parts of the distribution system for maintenance purposes.

The boiler has already been described and, for our purposes, there is no need to go further with an explanation of either the pump or the pipes and therefore we will go directly to the end of the system where the heat is delivered into the room and look at the various types of heating units.

HEATING UNITS

There are several types of heating units; these are characterized by their thermal performance and physical appearance. The thermal characteristics may be considered to have three components and these will be explained first.

METHODS OF TRANSFERRING HEAT

Heat is delivered to the room to be heated by one or more of three heat transfer mechanisms. These we met in the brief discussion about human comfort and they are: radiation, convection and conduction. The proportion of heat emitted in these various ways will depend upon the type of heating unit, but in the main radiation and convection will predominate. In the case of one type of unit the output may be predominantly radiant heat, while in another it is a combination of radiant and convection. This performance characteristic may be usefully employed in certain situations. For example, a sparsely populated warehouse, where there are frequent deliveries of material and the outside doors are rarely closed, may be most efficiently heated by radiant heat from an overhead source. However, the same method would not be as suitable in a well populated room which has a low ceiling, for reasons that will become obvious.

In addition to these characteristics there are two others which have a direct bearing on the choice of a unit for a particular problem. These are the speed of response to any change in the demand for heat, and the temperature gradient which is developed within the room by the unit.

THERMAL RESPONSE

The speed of response depends upon the mass of material that is in the heat transfer element, the volume of hot water passing through it, and the speed of the movement of the air over the heating element. This characteristic of the heating up, and also cooling down, of a particular type of unit should, like its fellows, be one of the determinants of choice, and needs to be matched to that of the activity of the occupants, the pattern of occupation and the thermal response of the room. Obviously if a room is to be heated quickly then a fast response is needed. Slightly less obvious is that this would be the same choice for a building that is of lightweight construction and intermittently occupied, and also for one that is designed to utilize passive heat gain. The preferred hierarchy of the time of response is that the system of control should be faster than that of the heater, which in turn should be faster than that of the room being heated.

TEMPERATURE GRADIENT

The vertical air temperature distribution, or temperature gradient, in a room is the combined effect of the type of heater, the temperature of the air leaving it, the shape of it and its planar orientation, and the standard of insulation of the building fabric. It is a performance characteristic that is of less importance now that buildings are being insulated to a higher standard and the surfaces of the room are not as cold, but still deserves care if the space has a tall volume and heat is not to be wasted. Fig. 5.1

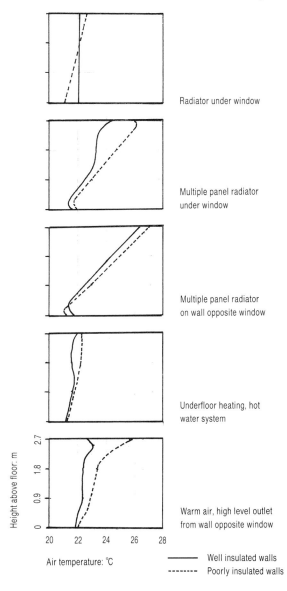

Radiator under window

Multiple panel radiator under window

Multiple panel radiator on wall opposite window

Underfloor heating, hot water system

Warm air, high level outlet from wall opposite window

Height above floor: m

Air temperature: °C

——— Well insulated walls
------- Poorly insulated walls

FIGURE 5.1 TEMPERATURE GRADIENTS OF HEATING UNITS (AFTER CALUWAERTS & MERRET)

FIGURE 5.2 TYPICAL PANEL RADIATOR

shows the temperature gradient produced by a typical radiator compared with that of an underfloor heating system. The shape of these will depend on where the heat is emitted into a room, together with how well the room is insulated (Goulding et al, 1993).

RADIATORS

Once again we meet a misnomer, for the 'radiator' is mainly a convector of heat. The typical radiator convects about 70% of its total heat output and the remainder is mostly radiated, although there may be a very small amount conducted directly to the surfaces in contact with its supports.

Radiators are made in a whole variety of shapes and sizes. There are two basic types, the familiar steel panel type with a ribbed surface (Fig. 5.2), or column which can now be made of cast aluminium, and, once more back in fashion, the cast-iron, columnar, sectional type once to be seen in every school in the land. The advantage of radiators is that they are simple, robust and easy to maintain. Their main disadvantage is that they have a slow thermal response time.

CONVECTORS

There are two types of convectors, the naturally convective and the forced convective. The central component of each of these is the heat exchange element, a simple pipe which has an extended

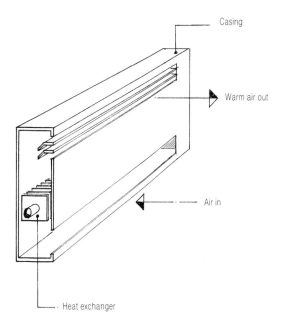

FIGURE 5.3 NATURAL CONVECTOR

surface area in the shape of fins or small plates of metal. Hot water from the distribution system passes through the pipe, heating both it and the extended surfaces. The convector element is in some form of enclosure, Fig. 5.3. Room air is induced into the bottom of the enclosure and, on passing over the finned pipe, becomes heated and buoyant before passing out at the top of the enclosure and into the room.

Convectors are generally mounted at sill or skirting level, and the enclosure can be made of metal or may be of a moulded plastic; it could also be a builder's work casing or part of a piece of furniture, e.g. the back of a work bench etc. In effect the vertical enclosure acts as would a chimney, and the taller it is the more brisk is the air movement over the heating element; this increases the heat transfer rate and therefore the heat output of the unit. Natural convectors have a fairly rapid response and produce a high heat output by comparison with physical size, in the range 0.5 to 4kW per metre length.

The forced convection unit has an improved response time and its heat output is improved by the addition of an electrical fan, Fig. 5.4. A unit such as this is often known as a fan-coil unit and may be used in a variety of ways. The diagram shows that one alternative to simply recirculating the room air through the unit is to introduce outside air and to mix this with a recirculated portion. They are capable of high heat outputs in the range 1.5 to 25.5kW. There are two main disadvantages, the first is that the fan can be noisy, especially when running at its highest speed, and the second is that it may produce a steep temperature gradient, giving rise to complaints about cold feet and over-warm heads. The way to lessen the risk is to select units that can offset the loss of heat at low speeds and with acceptably low outlet temperatures.

They have been much used in the design of school buildings. Apart from the familiar free-standing unit, quite often installed at one end of the classroom next to the chalkboard, slim-line models were developed for the system-built schools such as CLASP and SCOLA. These were designed to be suspended in the roof space and have a number of stub outlets from which warm air can be ducted to various places within the classroom.

In the main, fan-coil units are designed to fully recirculate the air in the room, but it is possible to adapt them so they may take in a proportion of outside air and mix this with recirculated air. The unit may be thermostatically controlled by a temperature sensing device in the room, and they are capable of being time controlled; as such they are very useful for rooms that are intermittently occupied.

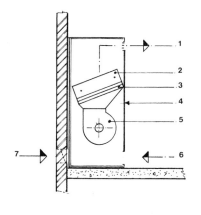

1 Warm air leaving unit
2 Heat exchanger ('coil')
3 Air filter
4 Casting
5 Fan
6 Room air entering unit
7 Alternative outside
 air entry

FIGURE 5.4 FAN-COIL UNIT

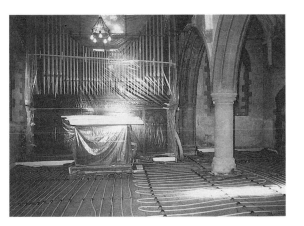

FIGURE 5.5 A LOW TEMPERATURE HOT WATER
UNDERFLOOR HEATING SYSTEM

RADIANT PANELS

Perhaps the greatest advantage of this method of heating a space is that comfortable conditions can be obtained without it being necessary to heat the whole of the occupied volume. This is because radiant heat can be beamed directly at the occupants; in effect the source heats whatever it 'sees' and does not heat the air in the space directly. The air temperature only increases by coming in contact with the surfaces that are first heated by the radiant energy. Therefore the heating effect is felt by the occupants even though the air in the room may be at a temperature below the acceptable norm. Radiant panels fall into two main classes:

● the exposed type,
● the enclosed panel, usually an integral part of the structure.

The exposed panel can be somewhat crude in appearance, being comprised of a metal tube or tubes, fixed to a steel panel, the back of which may be insulated. Hot water, or steam, is circulated through the tubes so that both they and the backing panel are heated. The heat being emitted is not wholly radiant, the proportion of radiant to convected heat being dependent upon how the panel is mounted; the radiant fraction will be at a maximum when the panel is in a horizontal plane. Discomfort can result if a radiant panel is too close to the people it is to heat, particularly if it has a high surface temperature, and therefore care is needed in choosing its position. The use of this type of unit

has decreased in favour of the direct fired radiant tube, which is reviewed later in this chapter.

The enclosed panel offers invisibility, among other things, and a floor completely free of any intrusive heating unit. Although panel heaters can be integrated within any part of the building's surfaces, the type most used are those that lie within the floor slab. Previous underfloor heating systems depending upon metallic hot water pipes were not always trouble-free, and as a result fell into disuse because they quite often sprung a leak that was not detected until much damage had been done. In the latest systems, however, the hot water flows through leak-proof unjointed loops of polyethylene pipes set within a fairly thin floor slab, the thickness of which is generally 50 mm and is insulated on its underside and at all exposed perimeter edges, Fig. 5.5. Although there are some limitations to the choice of material for the floor finish, hard surfaces such as quarry tiles being most suitable, manufactures claim that it is also possible to obtain good effects with light carpets and even suspended wooden floors.

Underfloor heating systems such as these are most suited to tall volumes such as churches, foyers and other places where there is little space available for other types of units, although their response time is improved by the relatively thin floor slab, unlike the thick slabs of the floors heated by off-peak electricity that are designed as storage heaters. However, even with this improved performance it works best when matched with the even demand of a heavyweight building and a fairly constant heating regime. The temperature of the water flowing through the network of pipes is usually no higher than 40 degrees C. This prevents any discomfort, particularly to those who spend much of their time walking on the heated floor, and makes it suitable for use in conjunction with a heat pump or solar panels where the outflow temperature is lower than that of a boiler. However, the down side is that the heat emission is low, and therefore if the heat loss which the system is required to offset is high then the uncovered floor area must be large. This can place a restriction on the placement of furniture. In addition the system is vulnerable to any future fixtures that penetrate the floor slab.

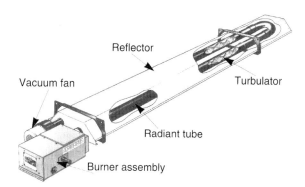

Reflector

Vacuum fan

Turbulator

Radiant tube

Burner assembly

FIGURE 5.6 GAS FIRED RADIANT TUBE (BY COURTESY OF AMBI-RAD LTD)

DISTRIBUTION AND THE VARIOUS SYSTEMS

Because each of the types of heating methods reviewed above have a different emission factor, and also because the underfloor system runs at a lower temperature (the surface temperature of the floor generally being below that of the skin) than any of the others, it is not advisable to mix any of them on the same distribution circuit. In particular, a mixture of radiators and fan convectors will cause difficulty with their thermal control and must be avoided (CIBSE, 1970, Section B1, Table B1.39).

DIRECT FIRED PACKAGED UNITS

There are many situations where the individual, independent unit is to be preferred to the centralized distributed installation. Typical of these are the single-volume industrial building, or the temporary office and school room. And, with the possible exception of the underfloor system, the individual units offer the same methods of heating a space as do their fellow units of the distributive installation.

DIRECT FIRED WARM AIR UNITS

In essence these are very simple; they consist of an enclosed combustion chamber in which either gas or oil is burnt under controlled conditions. Surrounding this is a second chamber through which the air to be heated passes; the air is usually driven by an electrical fan. In its action this is similar to the forced convective operation of the fan-coil unit, but

instead of a heating element with water from a boiler passing through it there is a furnace being directly heated by fuel. Most of the homes in North America are heated in this way, but the method has never been as popular in the UK. The situation may change because the gas fired units now available are much more efficient and quieter in operation than those that were in use a few years ago.

The units may be either floor-mounted or slung from the roof members. In most situations they are totally recirculative, the room air being recycled over the combustion chamber, but it is possible to adapt the operation so that a measure of fresh outside air may mix with that being recirculated. All the units need a chimney of some sort and a connection to a supply of fuel; they are therefore in no way mobile.

Their main advantages are of costs, ease of installation, and of being dismantled for use elsewhere, together with a reduced need for space. Although they have a fast response time they can also tend to develop a steep temperature gradient, due to the high air leaving temperature, and noise can also be a problem.

DIRECT FIRED RADIANT UNITS

There are several types of direct fired radiant units:

- Gas fired plaques that operate at 900 degrees C. These are unflued units not too dissimilar in principle to the domestic gas fire.
- Gas fired radiant tubes that operate at temperatures in the range 400 to 500 degrees C.
- In addition, but not strictly direct fired, are high temperature electric quartz heaters.

For obvious reasons it is not advisable to install any unflued unit, such as the gas fired plaque, in an occupied area unless there is a good flow of outside air passing through the space.

Direct fired radiant tubes are designed to exhaust the flue gases directly to outside and are particularly useful for large, enclosed volumes with long span structures where there is a need to keep the floor clear. They therefore find most use in industry, exhibition halls and sports centres, being particularly preferred in the latter to forced warm air units because they do not affect the flight of the shuttlecocks used in the game of badminton.

Radiant tubular heaters are simple in construction and operation. A gas burner fires directly into a metal tube, and a metal trough reflector fixed above the heated tube directs the radiant heat from its surface down to the occupants below; the products of combustion are then discharged to outside through a flue, Fig. 5.6. Their normal heat output is in the range 9.75 to 13.2kW, although it is possible to extend the total output of an installation by connecting several units together, Fig. 5.7. Obviously, because they are direct fired and operate at high temperatures, they must be kept away from any combustible material and mounted at a height that will not cause discomfort; the minimum mounting height of the smallest unit is therefore usually about 3.0 metres.

SUMMARY

All the units we have reviewed can form part of a modest heating system. Many need to work in conjunction with natural ventilation or a mechanical ventilation system that is designed to provide only the required ventilation rate. The latter combination of the two systems has come to be called 'mixed mode'.

The mixed mode method may be applied to any type of building, with some exceptions as has been outlined earlier – for example, the headquarters office building of the National Farmers' Union and Avon Insurance Group, Stratford upon Avon. Unlike many other prestige headquarters buildings, it is not fully air-conditioned. A major design objective was to make the best use of the outside climate, to give as much control as possible over the indoor

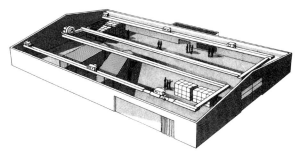

FIGURE 5.7 SCHEMATIC OF CONTINUOUS RADIANT HEATING SYSTEM (BY COURTESY OF AMBI-RAD LTD)

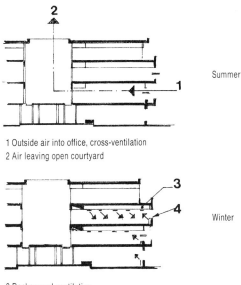

1 Outside air into office, cross-ventilation
2 Air leaving open courtyard

3 Background ventilation
4 Convectors heating office

FIGURE 5.8 MIXED MODE: NFU AND AVON INSURANCE HQ

environment to the occupants, and to limit the need for electrical power. Comfort conditions are maintained throughout the year by a combination of natural and mechanical ventilation systems, together with convector units at the building perimeter, the mixed mode.

During the heating season the convectors around the perimeter are supplied with low pressure hot water by the central boilers. The temperature of the water is controlled in step with the weather outside (known as being 'weather compensated'), but each convector has a thermostatic control valve that allows the occupants some further control to suit their own particular needs. Background ventilation is supplied by a mechanical system, the fresh air content of which is controlled by measuring the carbon dioxide content as the air is extracted from the offices; at this time the windows are kept closed. Out of the heating season, windows at high level are opened as necessary around the external perimeter, as well as those that face on to an inner open courtyard, to provide cross-ventilation, Fig. 5.8. Night-time cooling of the inside fabric of the building is made possible, without the security risk posed by open windows, by running the mechanical ventilation system (Nelson & Stamp, 1984).

Each type of unit has something to offer and will be found to be particularly suited to a given problem. Some buildings will require more than one type of unit, so resist the caution of those who say that it is best to use only one throughout. Their caution may be founded on the need to provide separate distribution circuits to suit the different emission characteristics and it may aim to reduce complexity and cost. It is now more usual to have several quite separate distribution networks, each serving a zone, and being designed to respond more readily to the needs of the zone so that energy may not be used unnecessarily.

The beginning of this chapter introduced the concept of the 'thermal form' of the building, suggesting that choosing a heating unit was more than simply ensuring that sufficient heat was supplied to offset the heat loss. You should now realize that it is the way in which the heat is delivered to meet a particular heating problem that is important. First identify the problem and then seek the best performance and physical characteristics to resolve it.

CHAPTER SIX

MECHANICAL VENTILATION SYSTEMS AND WARM HEATING

WHERE IS MECHANICAL VENTILATION NEEDED?

Real ventilation is so uncommon that ... the architect usually thinks this object has been attained if some of the windows can be opened. Some think that the presence of 'ventilators', especially if they have long names and are secured by 'Her Majesty's letter patent', ensures the required end. We may as well supply a house with water by making a trap door in the roof to admit rain.

Notes on the Ventilation and Warming, Professor Ernest Jacob, 1894.

It is unfortunate that this somewhat disparaging comment about nineteenth century architects and their apparent ignorance of the basic principles of ventilation still holds true for many twentieth century architects. In Chapter Two natural ventilation was shown to have certain limits to its effective application; when these limits apply then it is necessary to recognize the fact and to look to an alternative method, even though that method may mean that it is more demanding of energy. Too often the use by architects of the word 'natural' in association with light and even heat, as well as ventilation, and also to 'artificial' light, heat and ventilation, has moralistic overtones that are similar to the occasional dilemma over the proper application of certain materials of construction in some situations. The hard facts of the matter are these. The differences between natural and mechanical ventilation are that the first can be less demanding of energy, while the latter, if properly designed, is reliable even if the wind is blowing from the wrong direction. Morality does not come into it, client satisfaction does.

We have already seen that natural ventilation will not provide satisfactory results if certain conditions prevail, for example the building may have too deep a plan depth, or the outside climate may be too polluted, etc. On the other hand, it maybe physically possible to naturally ventilate a space, but the activity or function may be such that either opening the windows is impracticable, or there is a need to provide a dependable rate of air movement at all times. A typical example is the room that is used for presentations of some form, e.g. seminars and lectures, where there will be a need from time to time for it to be darkened so that slides or films may be shown and the windows will be closed or at least covered by blinds; effective natural ventilation would then be unlikely. Too many rooms are used like this in colleges up and down the country, to the disadvantage of speakers and listeners alike. What is needed is a simple ventilation system, but, as will be explained, one extract fan in a window will not do. In addition to these limitations to the use of natural ventilation that make the alternative method necessary, there are also situations, functions and activities that demand 100% reliability, despite the weather or wind direction, and for those only mechanical ventilation will do.

MECHANICAL VENTILATION SYSTEMS

The function of a mechanical ventilation system is the same as that provided by natural means, and that is to satisfy the requirement for ventilation which is defined succinctly by the Chartered Institution of Building Services Engineers (CIBSE) as: 'the amount of outdoor air needed to be supplied to a space to meet criteria associated with the use of that space' (CIBSE, 1970, Section B).

You will have no doubt realized by now that some mechanical ventilation systems may perform several duties. They may simply satisfy the requirement for ventilation, but in addition they may also serve to warm the building and also supply conditioned air as part of an air-conditioning installation. We will discuss these other duties later; for now, though, we will look at the components of the various mechanical ventilation systems and their function. There are three variations on the theme:

● Exhaust ventilation only, with a supply of replacement air by natural means.
● Input of air only, the exhaust air finding its own way out of the ventilated space.
● The balanced supply and extraction of air by an integrated system, which is sometimes called the 'plenum system'.

EXHAUST VENTILATION

This method is very basic and consequently limited in its application. Its most crude form is when a space is said to be ventilated by placing an extract fan in a window or wall opening. The idea being, presumably, that the fan will draw air from all parts of the room in equal measure and that air from outside will move into the room and be similarly distributed. However, it has been shown that the effectiveness on the general pattern of movement of the ambient air in a room of a point source of suction, such as that of the entrance opening into the extract fan, is limited and is directly related to the shape of the opening (CIBSE, 1970, Section B2-10). What this means is that when the air moving towards the fan opening is at a distance from it equal to the opening diameter, its velocity will be

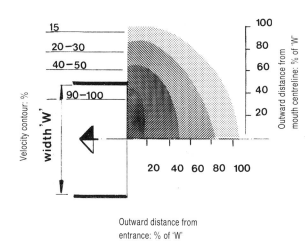

FIGURE 6.1 AIR MOVEMENT INDUCED BY AN EXTRACT POINT (AFTER CIBSE GUIDE BOOK B)

only 5% of that at the face of the entrance, Fig. 6.1. Although the simple extract system should, therefore, not be considered as being an effective means of ventilating a whole room, it can be usefully employed to remove an unwanted odour, a noxious gas, smoke or hot air. However, the opening to the extraction system must, for the reason given above, be positioned as close as possible to the source and take advantage of the physical characteristics of the contaminant.

KITCHENS

An extract hood over a range of kitchen appliances is a typical example of such an application, the warm buoyant air rising from the pots and pans and moving naturally towards the extract opening in the hood. Bear in mind that as the contaminated air is being extracted by the system more will move in to take its place. If this replacement air comes in directly from outside and is unheated it could be a nuisance. In such a situation it is better to either draw the air from another heated zone or heat the incoming air directly. If the kitchen serves a restaurant and is directly connected to it then the replacement air may come from the dining area, through the doors between the two rooms or permanent grilles; this method tends to have the advantage of keeping cooking smells within the kitchen. This method will not be possible when the kitchen is not connected to any other heated space, which is often the case with kitchens in a basement. If this is the situation then a positive replacement air supply must be provided, and it is usual to supply about 80 to 85% of the air volume being extracted. Although the kitchen may be self-sufficient in providing heat when all the ranges and ovens are working, it will be necessary to provide some background heat during the pre-cooking period.

The air change rate in kitchens can be high; it is recommended that at least 17.5 litres of air/second per square metre of floor area be extracted, this can mean an air change rate of 20 to 30 per hour (CIBSE, 1970, Section B2-20). The extract hoods, particularly those over frying pans, must be fitted with washable grease filters and made readily accessible for ease of cleaning; the build-up of grease increases an already great risk of fire. It is now usual to recover the heat from the extract air before it is discharged by a heat exchanger placed within the discharge duct.

UNDERGROUND CAR PARKS

Where it is not possible to ensure a brisk flow of air through an underground car park by natural means, i.e. there are less than two outside walls with openings in them less than 2.5% of the floor area, mechanical ventilation is required. The danger arises from the inflammable vapours leaking from the vehicles and the lethal carbon monoxide gas that leaves the car exhaust system. Recommended air change rates of between 6 to 10 per hour are usual, and it is advisable to extract the foul air close to the floor and at high level; stand-by fans are always necessary.

LAVATORIES AND BATHROOMS

Most local authorities will insist upon the provision of mechanical ventilation for public toilets. It is usual practice to extract 5 to 10 air changes per hour, although a minimum rate of 3 per hour would meet the minimum statutory requirements. The system will be quite simple; in a small single-storey building

individual fans operated from the light switch and having a time control device that allows the fan to run on for a few minutes after the toilet has been vacated would be sufficient. Multi-storey buildings, where the toilets on each floor are stacked directly above each other, can be served by one common extract duct connected to a unit on the roof containing two fans, one of which would be running and the other would be on stand-by.

SUPPLY VENTILATION

It has already been explained that the pattern of air movement within a room is dictated by the way in which it is introduced rather than the way air is extracted, and therefore in this respect the supply ventilation method is superior to that of the exhaust-only system. However, a ventilation system that only supplies air, there being no corresponding extraction of air, has a fairly limited application. It may be used to reduce the effects of an unwanted heat gain during the summer, by introducing outside air into a room to either cool the occupants directly or to mix with the air in the room and reduce the ambient air temperature to an acceptable level. Both methods are dependent for their efficacy upon the temperature of the outside air.

However, its application may be extended if the incoming air is warmed during the colder months so as not to cause a draught. Such an arrangement has the advantage of simplicity and may be based on the fan-coil unit that was described in the previous chapter. This unit can be arranged to draw in outside air and have it mix with a controlled proportion of air recirculated from within the room, and, although the power of the fan integral with the unit will not be sufficient to deliver the warm air through an extended duct system, the output would be quite enough for one or two moderate size rooms, such as those in teaching establishments.

Decentralized units, not unlike the fan-coil unit in principle, but much more sophisticated in operation, have found use in both industrial and commercial buildings that have large volumes and heights up to 13 metres. Some of these are not only capable of supplying a mixture of fresh and recirculated air, they also have the ability to recover heat from the vitiated air before it is discharged to

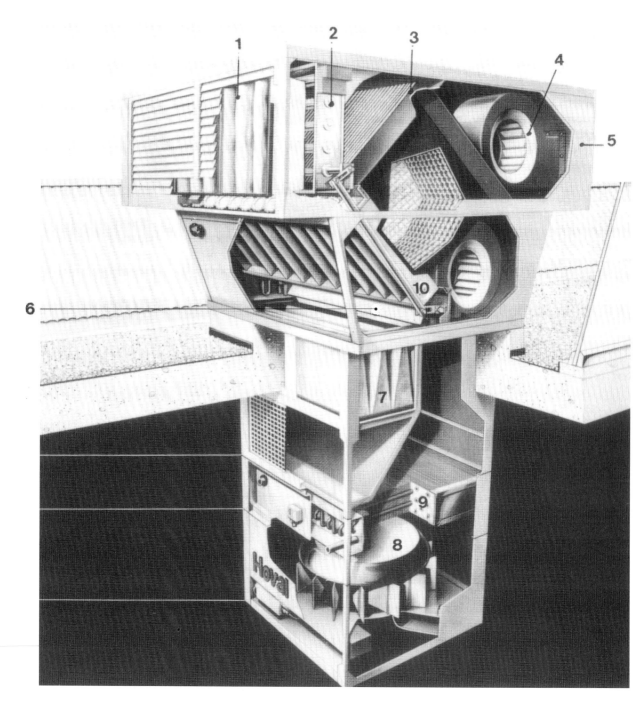

1 Air filter   6 Recirculation damper
2 Fresh air damper   7 Filter
3 Heat exchanger   8 Hoval air-injector
4 Fans   9 Heat exchanger
5 Casing   10 Bypass damper

FIGURE 6.2 WARM AIR UNIT MOUNTED ON ROOF (BY COURTESY OF HOVAL LTD)

atmosphere, Fig. 6.2. Recovering heat in this way can reduce energy costs, as an example: the manufacturer of one such unit found that the total heat loss of a factory was reduced by 41% due to the recovery of heat from the outgoing air. Fig. 6.3 illustrates the changes in operating mode which are possible, all of which are controlled automatically by time clocks and thermostats.

This type of operation is typical of such packaged units and may be extended during the summer to provide additional air movement, or be run at night to flush out the heat of the day and cool the fabric ready for occupation.

Air supply-only systems are finding greater use in the so-called 'mixed-mode' method of heating. This method has been referred to earlier in connection with the passive design of buildings and its use in conjunction with the simple heating system. In this method the heating system is usually based on radiators or warm convectors and designed to have an output that will offset the total loss of heat. The air supply system is designed to provide warm air, usually a few degrees above the temperature of the room (sometimes the air is said to be 'tempered', a nice old-fashioned description) and of a volume to be sufficient to meet the needs of the occupants in winter, it being assumed that where possible natural ventilation will be utilized in preference to the mechanical system when the heating is off. In many systems the rate at which the air is supplied is controlled by a carbon dioxide sensing device. The method offers the option of using the mechanical system during unseasonably hot weather to supplement natural ventilation.

BALANCED SYSTEMS

A balanced, or what is sometimes called a plenum system, is, as its title implies, designed to supply and extract a balanced volume of air through a distribution system of ducts. The air is supplied at a temperature above that of the room being heated and at a volumetric rate such that it will offset both the fabric and infiltration heat losses. In most situations there is no other form of heating to supplement the input, the exception being when there is an expanse of glass that may cause cold downdraughts; in this case heating units are placed

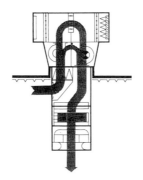

Pre-occupation Boost, full recirculation

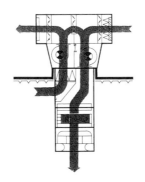

Mixed Air Operation, with heating

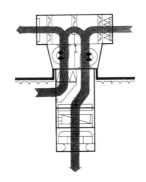

Mixed Air Operation, no heating

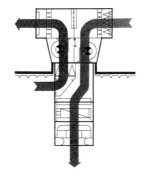

All Outdoor Air, no heating

FIGURE 6.3 OPERATING MODES, INDUSTRIAL VENTILATION (BY COURTESY OF HOVAL LTD)

below it to counteract the problem. It is important to realize that the volume of air being introduced into a room in order to offset the heat loss will, in most cases, be greater than that of the outdoor air supply.The combination of air volume and its temperature must be such that the heat content of the incoming air must be at least equal to that of the total heat loss, and there is a range of permutations of the proportions of volume to temperature that will make this so. A small volume of air combined with a high temperature would possibly suffice, but too high a temperature would cause an unsatisfactory temperature gradient and the occupants would experience the discomfort of cold feet and hot heads. Increasing the volume and reducing the temperature to below that required in the room would not do, either; in fact if you go back to Chapter Two you will recall that there is a relationship between air velocity, temperature and comfort.

There is, therefore, a need to choose the best combination that will suit the heat output required and human comfort. In general the necessary volume is obtained by mixing the incoming outdoor air with a percentage of recirculated air, the

proportions of which can be adjusted in accordance with the prevailing weather and the density of occupation: as a very generalized rule of thumb assume 5 to 6 air changes per hour, but be prepared to revise this if the building is poorly insulated, has altogether too much glass, is in an exposed position or the density of occupation is higher than normal (it is after all only a rule of thumb).

Where cooling and humidity control is not required, a system such as this can be extended to serve a whole building, providing all the necessary ventilation and heating throughout the year, or it can work in conjunction with other systems that are sufficient in their operation for other parts of the building. It will not provide the full environment control provided by the air-conditioning system, but it is capable of meeting the needs of many situations in the UK.

HEATING AND VENTILATING SYSTEMS

Central to a heating and ventilating installation is the air handling unit (AHU). Its function is to draw in air from outside, to filter out any solid pollutants, heat it to a controlled temperature and deliver the air into the distribution system. In most cases the AHU will also have the means of extracting the air from the return system. It has been referred to previously, but only in the sense of a 'black box', and now is the time to take a good look at it. You know already that it can demand quite a lot of room and that siting it does require some thought if it is to work properly. Air handling units can be made of a number of components, each one bought from a different manufacturer, or made by one company as a package of a series of modules that are assembled on site.

The components that make up the air handling unit have the same function no matter whether it is a package of modules or not. The number and type of components can be combined to meet specific duties and assembled to suit a wide field of applications, from the simpler ventilation unit for heating only to a complete one for full air-conditioning with heat recovery. Fig. 6.4 is a block diagram of the simpler unit; we will meet the more sophisticated

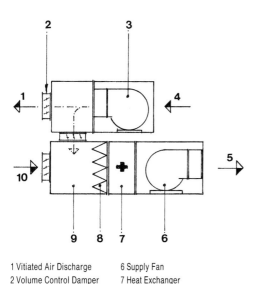

1 Vitiated Air Discharge	6 Supply Fan
2 Volume Control Damper	7 Heat Exchanger
3 Extract Fan	8 Filter
4 Return Air	9 Mixing Box
5 Warm Air Supply	10 Outdoor Air Entry

FIGURE 6.4 BLOCK DIAGRAM OF AIR HANDLING UNIT: HEATING ONLY WITH RECIRCULATION

type later when we discuss air-conditioning. The unit shown depicts a modular package. These are manufactured in a wide range of sizes, providing air outputs that are typically between 0.1 to 50 m³/second, and consisting of:

● An electrically driven fan to push the air through the supply ductwork.

● A similar fan to extract the air through the return ductwork.

● A filter to remove air-borne solid pollutants, the degree to which it does this being dependent on the application, a filter for say an operating theatre needing to remove a wider range of pollutants more efficiently than that for an auditorium.

● A heat exchanger, through which hot water from the centralized heating installation will be circulating and over which the air to be heated will be flowing. This will be thermostatically controlled.

● A mixing box and several volume control devices (commonly called 'dampers').

● Quite often, a heat recovery unit.

Heat is often recovered directly in part by recirculating part of the volume of air that is extracted from the room, the air being simply diverted by a system of automatically controlled devices (dampers), as shown in the diagram. However, the air being extracted from the room may be too foul or toxic to be mixed with the incoming air and yet its heat content may be too much to reject it as waste. In such a situation the remedy is to extract the heat from the air before it is discharged and to use that heat to give a boost to the incoming outside air. There are several ways of doing this:

● By installing what is known as a 'run-around-coil' in the ventilation system. This is a simple device of a heat exchanger in the extract air duct and another in that of the supply. The two are connected by a piped system through which water is pumped; there may be a need to add anti-freeze in some situations. The circulating water is heated as it passes through the heat exchanger in the extract duct and gives up the heat to the incoming air via the second heat exchanger, Fig. 6.5.

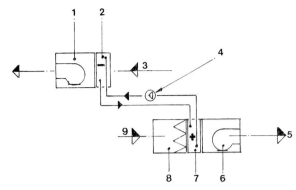

1 Extract Fan	6 Supply Fan
2 Heat Exchanger	7 Heat Exchanger
3 Return Air	8 Filter
4 Circulation Pump	9 Outdoor Air Entry
5 Warm Air Supply	

FIGURE 6.5 HEAT RECOVERY, RUN-AROUND-COIL

● Fig. 6.6 shows another method. In this a plate heat exchanger is placed between the extract air flow and the incoming air. This in its simplest form is a box in which there are a series of divisions so that the outgoing air flows on one side of a divider and the incoming moves over the divider on the other side. In this way the two air flows never meet and the heat of one passes to the other because the divider is warmed by the passage of the outgoing air stream. It has the advantage of having no moving parts.

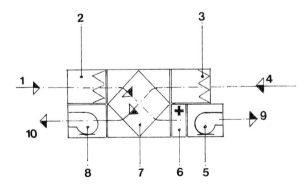

1 Outdoor Air Entry	6 Heat Exchanger
2 Filter	7 Plate Heat Exchanger
3 Filter	8 Extract Fan
4 Return Air	9 Warm Air Supply
5 Supply Fan	10 Vitiated Air Out

FIGURE 6.6 HEAT RECOVERY, PLATE HEAT EXCHANGER

● A variation of the second method is to arrange the box and its divisions in a wheel and to slowly rotate it through the two air streams so that parts are in one flow or the other, Fig. 6.7. As the wheel passes through the extract plenum chamber the air flows through the divisions, heating them as it goes. The now heated fill of the wheel rotates into the incoming air plenum and as the air flows through it it is heated in turn. To prevent any carry-over of solid pollutants there is usually a scavenging quadrant in the wheel scoured by a portion of the incoming air before the heated section moves into the incoming air plenum proper. The advantage of this over the plate exchanger is that it is more compact and the rate at which heat is exchanged may be controlled by the speed at which the wheel rotates.

● The most efficient method of all is to use a heat pump, the process of which has already been described, in place of the run-around-coil.

In an order of operating efficiency it is claimed that the run-around-coil is about 50% that of the plate exchanger and the wheel up to 75% and the heat pump as high as 90%; the order of cost is generally in reverse order.

The air handling unit will be connected to the distribution system, ducts will carry the warm air to where it is needed and there it will be blown into the room from some form of grille, louvre or diffuser. The vitiated air will be withdrawn from the space and pass along the return duct system back into the air handling unit, where it will either be recirculated in combination with some incoming outdoor air or discharged to atmosphere.

At this point you may wish to refer back to the space allocation diagram, Fig. 4.16; it should make a little more sense now and your design project could benefit from the exercise. Also, there are Design Exercises later, from which you see all the pieces coming together.

There is much more to it than that bald statement, but we will leave it there; for much of the detail is shared with that of the air-conditioning system and that is where we are heading next. Should you want to complete the picture of the heating and ventilating-only system do skip ahead and read about the methods of room air distribution in Chapter Eight. You can come back to air-conditioning later.

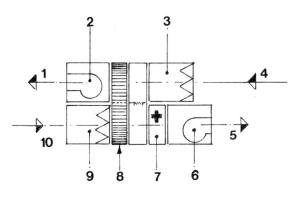

1 Vitiated Air Out	6 Supply Fan
2 Extract Fan	7 Heat Exchanger
3 Filter	8 Thermal Wheel
4 Return Air	9 Filter
5 Warm Air Supply	10 Outdoor Air Entry

FIGURE 6.7 HEAT RECOVERY, THERMAL WHEEL

CHAPTER SEVEN

AIR-CONDITIONING SYSTEMS

THE NEED FOR AIR-CONDITIONING

The Larkin administration building was a simple cliff of brick hermetically sealed (one of the first 'air-conditioned' buildings in the country) to keep the interior space clear of the poisonous gases in the smoke from the New York Central trains that puff along besides it.

Reyner Banham on Lloyd Wright's statement (Banham 1969, p. 86)

In his comment about Lloyd Wright's design of the Larkin building Banham makes several interesting points about the way in which Wright integrated the ventilation ducts and his 'judicious' claim that it was the first building to be air-conditioned; in fact, as Banham points out, he was not entirely correct. What is also interesting is Lloyd's reason for choosing air-conditioning, for it had not yet become the thing to do to attract higher rents, nor was he the harbinger of the hi-tech style. Instead he appears to have been motivated solely by the need to exclude the pollution caused by the passing trains.

Earlier than this, in 1894, an architect called William Henman had described the ventilation of hospitals by natural means as being 'impracticable' because of air pollution (Guedes, 1979). The solution he designed for Birmingham's New General Hospital was crude by today's standards, but advanced in its day, consisting of a fan driven system that drew air through hanging wetted ropes,

in an effort to remove some of the solid pollutants, before it was heated and delivered to the wards.

Air pollution is a valid reason for choosing to use an air-conditioning system as an alternative to ventilating a building by simply opening the windows. The pollution will result from the uncontrolled emission of the by-products of human activity, such as chemical waste from industrial processes and exhaust gases from motor vehicles; the list grows day by day, posing a threat to our health. There are also natural 'pollutants', the dust and pollens that may cause misery to some and be a positive nuisance to facility managers, yet go unnoticed by those who delight in the open window. Ironically the very use of air-conditioning can be the indirect cause of an increase in some of the pollutants it is designed to exclude.

Natural ventilation rather than mechanical, together with individual control of the indoor climate, is desirable if we wish to limit the environmental impact of buildings and their services. However, as was indicated in previous chapters, this is not always possible.

In the design of offices air-conditioning is seen as being not only necessary, because of the excess of heat caused by the machines and the lighting, but also as a Developer's *sine qua non*: 'an office building can't be rented if it isn't air-conditioned'. In the 1980s the plan depth of offices moved from about 12 metres to as much as 18 metres, to provide more flexibilty for a mixture of open plan and closed spaces, all uninterrupted by any through circulation. Floor to floor heights increased to provide more space for the mass of cables, pipes and ducts, and 3.6 to 4.5 metres became the norm. In the recession hit '90s the way offices are used is changing and a closer study has been made of the heat emission that was expected to cause a nuisance which showed it to be less than was expected (BSRIA, 1992a). Some observers of the situation are now of the opinion that the market over-reacted to the need for the IT office and its high technology and see a different role for the office designer. 'The design role of the 1990s will be less about accommodating and more about making places where creativity can thrive' (Worthington, 1992).

Despite these changes in advice and opinion there will still be a need for air-conditioning. That need may be the same as that identified by Lloyd Wright, or may be necessary to ensure clean conditions in an operating suite or computer centre; perhaps the climate may be too extreme, or it may be enforced by the shape of the site and the required accommodation.

AIR-CONDITIONING: ITS FUNCTION

What do we mean when a building is said to be air-conditioned? Air-conditioning is defined by the CIBSE as being: 'the supply and maintenance of a desirable condition of the atmosphere within a building despite any changes in the external climate or casual, internal gains'. This implies the control of air purity, temperature, and humidity, together with its speed and direction. With a few exceptions the desirable conditions are maintained by treating air which is later introduced into the conditioned room from some form of terminal unit. The aim is to offset any interchange of heat (the cooling, or heating, load) by either mixing the incoming conditioned air with that in the room, or by directly heating or cooling the occupants. The few exceptions rely on a radiant cooling effect and these we shall discuss later.

The required condition of the air before it is introduced into the room must obviously be a function of the cooling load referred to above, which is the sum of the heat and moisture either entering the room or being generated within it. However, the air-conditioning system must be capable of maintaining acceptable conditions throughout the year and therefore there may be a need to provide heating as well as cooling. A full air-conditioning system will therefore filter out some of the pollutants, cool and/or heat the incoming air, and adjust its moisture content.

THE COOLING LOAD

The cooling load has two constituent forms: sensible heat – attributable to differences in temperature and may be measured directly; latent heat – attributable to differences in moisture content and identified as a change of state. Sensible heat gains are the result of heat being given off by the occupants and any machines they may be operating, together with incoming solar gain through the fabric of the building, and the air being introduced from outside. Without the benefit of air-conditioning these gains would cause the indoor temperature to rise above an acceptable level.

Latent heat gains may be more difficult to comprehend. Remember that a change of state takes place without an apparent change in temperature, even though there is an output of heat. An everyday example is to be observed when water is boiled. When the water is first heated its temperature will rise, during this stage the amount of heat required is known as the 'sensible heat', its effect can be sensibly measured. Under normal conditions the water will boil when its temperature reaches 100 degrees C; if the heat input is maintained the water will continue to boil, and steam (water vapour) will be produced; leave the heat on and eventually all the water will have boiled away. The water has changed its state from a liquid to a gas; had you cared to measure its temperature while it was boiling you would have found that it remained at boiling point. The latent (or 'hidden') heat could have been measured following on from the sensible stage.

Although we can't see the water vapour being given off by the occupants of a room, which is just as well perhaps for the romantically inclined, it is there and is produced by their respiration and perspiration. In addition, moisture will arise from any manufacturing process, and the evaporation of water from drying clothes, or showers or pools. The incoming air will also carry its burden of moisture. All of these can combine to cause an unwelcome rise in the indoor humidity that could cause discomfort to the occupants, and distress amongst the micro-insides of computers.

An air-conditioning system has to be designed so that it is capable of delivering air into a room that will offset the combined effect of the sensible and latent heat gains (the proportion of sensible to latent heat gains is known as the 'room sensible heat ratio') but will not be perceived by the occupants as being an uncomfortable draught. It has to be said that this aim is not always achieved.

The study of the nature of moist air, so important to the design of air-conditioning, is known as 'psychrometry'. A not too detailed understanding of the laws that govern the behaviour of moist air can prove to be useful. In addition to helping you with these present studies it would also inform the diagnosis of such things as the risk of interstitial condensation in a construction you may have designed.

PSYCHROMETRY

We have already agreed, I hope, that the amount of moisture that may be held in a mass of air is related to the temperature of the air. When air is at a high temperature it will hold more moisture then when at a low temperature. But there is a maximum to the holding capacity, witness the 'steam' in the sauna, or the fog on the station platform. A mass of air that has reached this maximum point is said to be 'saturated'. Some idea of the amount of water vapour required to saturate air is given in Table 7.1.

Table 7.1. Moisture content of saturated air

Dry bulb temperature (°C)	Moisture content (kg/kg)
0	0.0003789
20	0.01475
40	0.04910

When air is said to be saturated its so-called 'dry bulb temperature' is equal to that measured by a dry bulb thermometer. You will no doubt have come across a wet bulb thermometer, so called because

its bulb is wrapped in a wick that is kept wet with water. The water in the wick evaporates under normal conditions and, because the heat for evaporation (i.e. the latent heat) is taken from the bulb, a drop in temperature is shown. If the air is saturated with moisture however, evaporation cannot take place and there will be no drop in temperature. And so, when there is a difference in the temperature of the dry and the wet bulb thermometer the air is not saturated, and when they are equal, it is.

You will also recognize the term 'humidity' and therefore also 'relative humidity'. Both refer to the moisture in the air, the latter being a comparison of the amount of moisture in the air with the maximum that could be held. This everyday definition is not strictly true, but is good enough for our present purposes. The important thing to recognize is that for a given moisture content the relative humidity of a mass of air depends upon its temperature.

For ease of reference all of this information can be shown on a particular type of diagram known as the psychrometric chart. The complete version of the chart does contain a lot of data and is used as a design aid. The first illustration of it, Fig. 7.1, is a slightly simplified version and shows the relation-

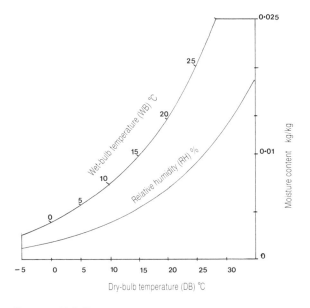

FIGURE 7.1 PSYCHROMETRIC CHART 1, SIMPLIFIED

ships we have covered so far. It indicates the dew point temperature, together with the saturation line and relative humidity. Given two bits of data it is possible with this form of graph to determine any of the other characteristics of the mass of air in question.

The more complex form of the psychrometric chart provides information about the sensible and latent heat together within the total heat content (more correctly called 'enthalpy') and it is possible to show on it all the processes that go on within an air-conditioning unit and to determine the changes in the heat content as a mass of air moves through a system. Note the protractor on the left giving the room sensible heat ratio; we will discuss its use shortly, Fig. 7.2

The aim of the next section is to provide you with an insight into the process of conditioning air as it goes through the various components of an air-conditioning system. It should help you to understand why some of the units are needed at some times and are not at others; if nothing else it will add to your technical vocabulary and improve communication at any multi-disciplinary design meeting. However, it you are in a hurry you may skip it for now and come back to it later.

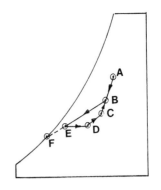
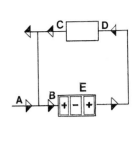

FIGURE 7.3 COMPLETE AIR CONDITIONING PROCESS

THE PROCESS OF CONDITIONING AIR

The air that is to be introduced into the rooms may be pre-conditioned in various ways in order to offset the sensible and latent heat gains; it may also be necessary to provide heat to make up for that lost through the building fabric. The heat gain in a room, for example, may be entirely one of sensible heat and therefore the incoming air would be cooled to offset it. However, the gain may be such that cooling the air reduces its moisture content below comfort level. In such a situation, the process would both cool the air and add moisture. On the other hand, there may be both sensible and latent heat gains; the process would then need to cool and dehumidify the air. A complete air-conditioning system will process the air through more than one of these cycles one after the other, each automatically controlled. These various processes can be shown on the psychrometric chart. Figure 7.3 shows a typical process. Air is drawn from outside and mixed with some of the air being extracted from the rooms. This saves energy but the quantity of air which may be recirculated depends upon the density of occupation and the activity of the occupants; in multi-cellular offices the recirculated air may be as much as 35% of the total delivered air volume. The process shown assumes that it is summer and the condition of the air outside is at 'A', this mixes with the air leaving the room 'C' to produce the condition at 'B'. The air then moves through a cooling and dehumidifying cycle, 'B'–'E', but at this stage the air

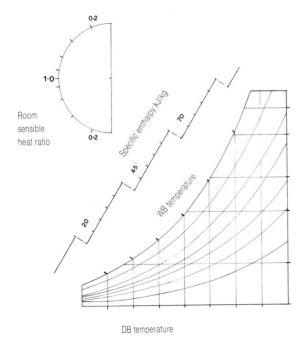

DB temperature

FIGURE 7.2 PSYCHROMETRIC CHART 2

would be too cool for comfort and therefore it is heated 'E'–'D' before leaving the conditioning unit and entering the room. Finally, the air enters the room and offsets the gains 'D'–'C'. Note the chain dotted line 'E'–'F', which indicates a measure of the efficiency of the cooling coil; the actual drop in temperature of the air as it passes over the coil is represented by point 'E'. If the heat transfer process going on through the coil had been 100% efficient then the air would have been cooled to point 'F' (this is known as the 'apparatus dew point').

It is possible to save energy by arranging a portion of the air volume to by-pass part of the cycle. Air may be ducted around the cooling/dehumidification cycle to mix later with the main volume and save the need for re-heating ('E'–'D').

We saw in Chapter Two that there is a relationship between comfort, and the speed and temperature of a moving mass of air: too low a temperature coupled with too high a speed, and discomfort will result. When providing cooling, the temperature of the incoming air must be lower than that already in the room, and the cooling effect must be equal to the cooling load; putting it somewhat unscientifically – the lack of heat in the one must equal the surplus in the other so that they balance each other out. The cooling effect can be achieved by several possible permutations of temperature and air volume, a lower temperature combined with a smaller air volume being the same as a higher temperature together with a higher volume.

Fixing the best permutation can be an iterative process. This may be assisted by using the room sensible heat ratio (RSHR). The slope of the line indicated by the RSHR protractor may be drawn on the psychrometric chart, representing the change in the condition of the air from leaving the air handling unit to it leaving the room. Point 'C' represents the desired condition of the room and the nearer 'D' is to it the smaller is the difference in the temperature of the air entering the room and that of the air leaving it. It follows that if the temperature difference is small the air volume must needs be larger, for a given cooling load. The volume of air to be delivered to the conditioned space will therefore not necessarily be equal to that required for ventilation alone; depending upon the occupation density it may often be

higher. The total volume may then be made up of a proportion coming in from outside mixed with a recirculated volume, as shown in the various diagrams.

THE SYSTEM

You will realize that all air-conditioning systems need a means of cooling the air and that this will inevitably call for refrigeration of some form. We have already covered in a broad form the subject of refrigeration in Chapter Four and now we will look at its application to the various air-conditioning processes.

There are two main types of systems, the 'Direct Expansion' system (DX) and what is sometimes called the 'Hydronic' (i.e. water-based) system, or central plant, both of which have their advantages and disadvantages and are appropriate for some uses and not for others. Generally speaking the choice for the larger building with a single tenant is the centrally based hydronic system that provides cooling for the whole building, or a similar but partially decentralized arrangement where the refrigeration set serves air handling plants adjacent to a zone. The DX system is more likely to be chosen for the multi-tenanted building or where only part of the building is to have air-conditioning; it is often used in the refurbishment of offices where space is limited and the location of central plant has proved to be impossible.

DIRECT EXPANSION SYSTEM

This type of unit is usually most suited to the smaller cooling load and is the basis of the self-contained air-conditioning system. You will remember from Chapter Four that the vapour compression refrigeration cycle has two heat exchangers, one of which absorbs heat – the evaporator, and the purpose of the other is to discharge that heat – the condenser. Through both of these flows the refrigerant that is the heat transfer medium. In the direct expansion system the air that is to be cooled flows directly over the evaporator, giving up this heat to the refrigerant and causing it to evaporate and expand – hence the title direct expansion system.

Such units may be packaged in one casing and installed within the room to be cooled, or sometimes, particularly in North America, in a window opening, where they are liable to drip condensate on to the unsuspecting passer-by. Banham (1969) gives an entertaining and informative description of the development of the American domestic air-conditioning unit, saying that it was originally known as the air-conditioning equivalent to Henry Ford's Model 'T' motor car or 'Flivver'. These are not capable of providing complete air-conditioning; their purpose is to cool the air and although some dehumidification may occur when the cooling load is heavy, there is no integrated means of adding moisture. In that the compressor is part of the unit there is a definite risk of the noise it generates causing a nuisance. The package is often split into two parts, the noisier section being put outside or in some less noise-sensitive space.

Because these packaged units offer only a limited conditioning effect they are most often used for what is described as 'comfort cooling', which is at best a convenient marketing term. Despite this limitation the system has developed to become a serious alternative to the central plant installation, becoming known as the 'multi-split' system capable of serving many units in zones scattered throughout a building. These larger systems can provide a flexibility to meet any change in building use, and, because they are essentially a decentralized unit, they suit a phased development programme and a group of individual tenants whose working hours differ. Advocates of the system, largely the manufacturers, claim that there is a definite trend away

from central plant and point to the Heathrow Sterling Hotel as an example, where there are no fewer than 450 fan-coil units.

Perhaps the most serious, topical disadvantage of the DX system is that it relies far more upon refrigerant as a heat transfer medium than do the central plant systems, which on balance use less refrigerant and more water. The greater the use of refrigerant the greater the risk of its escape to atmosphere and therefore the greater the risk of environmental impact. It is also argued that maintenance costs are bound to be higher, largely because of the need for higher-skilled personnel to handle pipework carrying refrigerant, and that the central plant is no more demanding for space than the DX system (Love, 1992).

[See Table 7.2. Figures for hydronic plant are for a roof-mounted air-cooled chiller. Plant space does not include servicing or access space. The figures do not include indoor units. (Information from Carrier Air Conditioning).]

CENTRAL PLANT SYSTEM

The fundamental difference between this method and the DX system is that the cooling effect brought about by the refrigeration unit is passed on to water, and this is the final heat transfer medium, rather than the total dependence of the DX unit on refrigerant to carry the cooling effect. This explains the more North American title of the hydronic system.

Table 7.2. Plant space for hydronic and multi-split air-conditioning systems

	Building Size (m²)	Cooling Capacity (kW)	Number of Chillers	Number of DX systems	Plant Space (m²)
Hydronic	1000	100	1		3
DX			—	4	3.5
Hydronic	2500	250	1–2 circuits	—	7.94
DX			—	9	7.95
Hydronic	5000	500	1–2 circuits	—	15.18
DX			—	18	15.9
Hydronic	10000	1000	1–2 circuits	—	17.7
DX			—	35	30.9
Hydronic	20000	200	2	—	35.4
DX	—	—	—	69	61

In this system the evaporator is associated with a second heat exchanger, water is pumped through the latter and is chilled by the indirect contact with the refrigerant and then circulated on through a distribution system. It is this chilled water that provides the cooling for the air handling units and the other types of units that comprise the complete air-conditioning system.

We have previously covered the primary means of providing full air-conditioning: boilers to give heat, and refrigeration to cool and modify the humidity of the air. There are many ways of delivering these primary means to the spaces to be conditioned; with some exceptions these fall into two broad groups, one being known as the 'all-air system; and the other as the 'air-water system'. With the first group the total heating and cooling load uses only air as the heat transfer medium, while the second one divides the load into two parts using both chilled or heated water and conditioned air and circulates these to the rooms, Fig. 7.4.

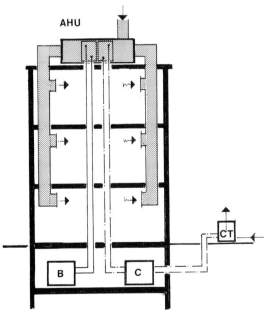

AHU

AHU: Air Handling Unit
B: Boilers
C: Chiller
CT: Cooling Tower

FIGURE 7.4 BLOCK DIAGRAM OF THE COMPONENTS OF ALL-AIR AND AIR-WATER AIR-CONDITIONING SYSTEMS

ALL-AIR SYSTEMS

The all-air system is an appropriate choice where the occupation density is high and there is a need for a corresponding high ventilation rate, an auditorium would be a typical example. It is also the answer to the problem space where there is a high cooling load in a deep space, and particularly where the latent heat is significant.

It is obviously necessary to offset any changes in the cooling load by changing either the condition of the incoming air or its volume, and this may be done in a variety of ways depending upon the size of the zone served and the number of different rooms in it.

CONSTANT AIR VOLUME, SINGLE DUCT

This is the most simple variation and is most suited to a single-volume zone, or a number of rooms that have similar, steady cooling load characteristics. The condition of the air will be controlled by sensing devices mounted either in the return air duct (in this way they sense a rough average condition of the space) or in the room itself.

Where there are several rooms served by the same system it is most difficult to provide one common incoming conditioned supply that equally satisfies all the rooms; only an unsatisfactory compromise condition is possible. The result would be particularly unsatisfactory in a zone where some of the rooms have a northern aspect and the others a southerly one. This has often been the case and the solution adopted was to cool the air down to meet the worst case and provide local reheaters that were controlled individually, Fig. 7.5. Such a method is bound to be wasteful and is not now recommended.

Space Allocation: see the duct sizing diagram.

ALL-AIR MULTI-ZONE

The alternative to this is to mix the air at the air handling unit and then circulate the resulting mix in one duct. To do this the air handling unit has what is known as a 'hot deck', in which there is a heat exchanger, and a 'cold deck' which has within it a chiller and possibly the means of adjusting the moisture content. These so called multi-zone systems require a lot more space for the ductwork

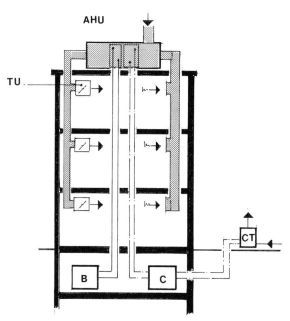

AHU: Air Handling Unit
  B: Boilers   CT: Cooling Tower
  C: Chiller   TU: Terminal Unit

FIGURE 7.5 ALL-AIR SINGLE-DUCT

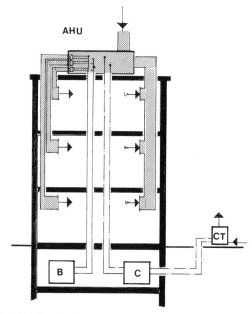

AHU: Air Handling unit with multi-zone reheat
  B: Boilers
  C: Chiller
  CT: Cooling Tower

FIGURE 7.6 ALL-AIR MULTI-ZONE

adjacent to the air handling units and it is best to restrict their use to a small number of zones, Fig. 7.6. Space Allocation: as single-duct system.

ALL-AIR DUAL-DUCT

In a dual-duct system the control of conditions is achieved by mixing a volume of cool air from one duct with that of warm air from another before it is introduced into the room, the mixture being controlled thermostatically, Fig. 7.7. This means that paired ducts run side by side throughout the building, serving each room in a zone, and it is both expensive and demands much more space than any single-duct system.
Space Allocation: each duct carries about 65% of the equivalent all-air, single-duct system.

ALL-AIR, VARIABLE AIR VOLUME

The most versatile and popular system to serve a variety of numerous zones is the variable air volume system. Whereas the systems we have covered so far have achieved control by holding the air volume

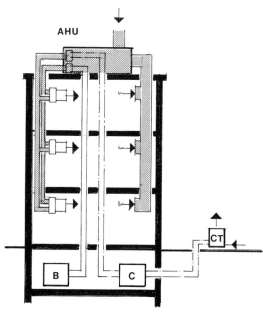

AHU: Air Handling unit with hot & cold decks
  B: Boilers
  C: Chiller
  CT: Cooling Tower

FIGURE 7.7 ALL-AIR DUAL-DUCT

steady and varying the air temperature, this method does the reverse, the air volume is varied and the condition of the incoming air is held constant.

A basic variable air volume system has the disadvantage that a single system cannot cope with a wide range in the simultaneous demand for heating and cooling. This problem may be overcome with the addition of local cooling and reheat units. Also, because the air volume varies, the way in which air is introduced into a room is changed and may not be properly distributed. It is possible to ensure that this does not happen by automatically mixing the incoming air with recirculated room air to maintain the volume handled by the louvres, or by installing fan-powered mixing boxes in the space. The mixing boxes are supplied with the conditioned air and mix this with a proportion of recirculated air before it is introduced into the room, Fig. 7.9.

Space Allocation: the terminal unit is usually installed horizontally above a suspended ceiling, either in the room or above an adjoining corridor. The size depends on the area of the zone it serves and is in the range 200 to 450 mm deep and can have a maximum length of 1.500 metres.

AIR-WATER SYSTEMS

In this method a volume of outdoor air, sufficient to meet the ventilation requirements related to occupation density, is conditioned in an air handling unit and circulated at a high velocity through small ducts to a terminal unit in the room. This so-called 'primary air' enters the terminal unit where it is mixed with a proportion of recirculated air, known as 'secondary air,' before entering the room. There are two types of terminal units, one being fan-powered and the other relying on induction.

Space Allocation: the velocity of the air is usually between 10 to 20 m/s; see the appropriate duct sizing diagram.

FAN-COIL UNIT

In principal this unit is similar to the simple warm air unit we discussed earlier. It has an electrically powered fan, a coarse filter and a heat exchanger all housed in a casing; the main difference is that there is a connection for the primary air, Fig. 7.8.

There are several variations possible, all of which

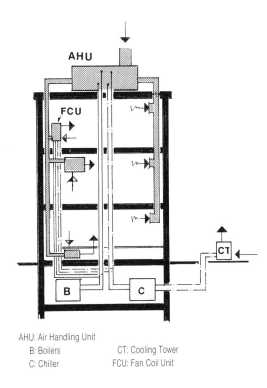

AHU: Air Handling Unit
B: Boilers   CT: Cooling Tower
C: Chiller   FCU: Fan Coil Unit

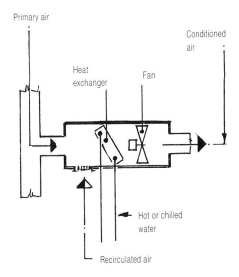

Fan Coil Unit

FIGURE 7.8 AIR-WATER SYSTEM

concern the heat exchanger. The fan draws the mixture of primary and secondary air over the heat exchanger, where it may be heated or cooled to suit the needs of the room. In the most basic unit the heat exchanger receives either hot or chilled water,

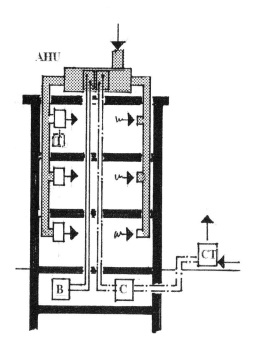

AHU: Air Handling Unit
B: Boilers   TU: VAV Terminal
C: Chiller   T : Room Thermostat
CT: Cooling Tower

FIGURE 7.9 VARIABLE AIR VOLUME

depending on the season: the 'two-pipe system'. Such a method may be suitable for a country that has clearly demarked seasons, but would be far too crude for many. A better alternative is to supply both hot and cold water to the unit and to have the flow controlled by a room-mounted thermostat. This means that the unit would be connected to four hose pipes, hence the 'four-pipe system'.

The main advantage of this system comes from the way in which the load is split between two types of heat transfer media, and it is that the volume of air being circulated is only about one quarter of that carried by the all-air method. It is most used in office buildings and other rooms that have similar low occupational densities and where the latent heat load is not high, such as hotel bedrooms. In offices the units are generally arranged around the peri-meter, although there is a growing trend of a move away from this position as walls become more energy efficient.

Space Allocation: the fan-coil unit is often designed to fit below the window sill, and in general even

those that are not are about the same size: 600–700 mm high, 250–300 mm deep, the length depends on output.

INDUCTION UNITS

The main difference between this unit and the fan-coil unit is that the room air is drawn in by induction. Primary air is brought in at high velocity through a nozzle, which causes a Venturi effect, lowering the static pressure in its vicinity and thereby drawing in the secondary, recirculated air.

It has the advantage that it does not require fan power in the unit, but this is offset by the need to pressurize the air somewhat before it enters; there is also the risk of a noise nuisance being caused by the air leaving the nozzle. This method has gener-ally lost favour to the advantage of the fan-coil unit. Space Allocation: about the same as the fan-coil unit.

ALTERNATIVE METHODS

In addition to the two most-used methods there are some fringe systems that are gaining in popularity for various reasons. One of these uses the principle of the heat pump and the others are variations on the air-water method.

UNIT HEAT PUMPS

We have already discussed the heat pump's ability to switch roles and to make use of low-grade heat; these characteristics may be used to good effect in a unitary air-conditioning installation. A unit heat pump may be used in a building where there is a surplus of heat in one zone and underheating in another, absorbing the surplus, enhancing it and emitting it where it is needed.

Several independent units may be connected together by a closed circuit system of pipes through which is circulated water at a constant temperature. The individual heat pumps will either be giving heat to the circulating water or transferring heat from it; depending on the condition of the room it serves, and the water will be kept at a constant temperature by central plant equipment.

In a similar way to the air-water system the unitary heat pump does not supply the outdoor air necessary for ventilation and does need to be supplemented by a mechanical ventilation scheme.

Space Allocation: like the fan-coil unit the unitary heat pump is designed principally to be free-standing below the window sill; it is slightly bulkier with a depth of about 300 mm.

PANEL SYSTEMS

These are also a variation on the air-water principle because they too are designed to split the total load so that the circulating water carries the sensible load and the air takes care of the latent heat gain. They have the similar, if slightly less, advantage of the fan-coil unit in that their use gives a 50% reduction in the circulated air volume by comparison to the all-water method.

Heat from the occupants and the other sensible gains is radiated to chilled water pipes carried above either a perforated metal ceiling or long metal planks. They have the advantage that they can be concentrated above localized 'hot spots', and the whole room may be sub-divided to provide a perimeter zone where the heat loss may be greatest during the winter and an inner zone where there is a heat gain throughout the year.

Their main disadvantage is that they cannot cope with any sudden changes in air humidity, otherwise condensation may occur on the cooled surfaces; careful control of the temperature of the circulating water is necessary for the same reason.

Unlike all other systems considered so far the panel method does need a separate ventilation system. In many instances the system is coupled with what is now known as 'displacement ventilation', that is introducing air at low level and at temperatures only a few degrees lower than that of the room air – this is described in more detail in the following chapter.

A different application of the method was installed in the building designed by Erskine known as The Ark, Fig. 7.10. In this, water at a mean temperature of about 15 degrees C is circulated through cooled convective elements above a metal slatted ceiling. Cooled currents of air drop through the ceiling to the occupied space below to offset the heat gains. Warm air from the room, and particularly off the glazing, rises up through wooden edge slats at the perimeter of the ceiling, cooling and dropping as it passes over the convective elements. When it is needed, heat is provided by radiant panels set at the edge of the ceiling.

The next chapter deals with the distribution of air for simply ventilating a space, or providing heating and ventilation, or air-conditioning. It is a description of the final connection between the main components that provide heating and cooling and the end user.

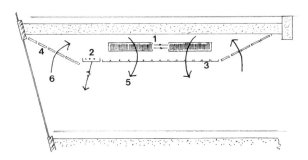

1 Convective cooling element	4 Ceiling edge slats
2 Radiant heating panel	5 Descending cool air
3 Metal slats of ceiling	6 Rising warm air

FIGURE 7.10 THE ARK

CHAPTER EIGHT

AIR DISTRIBUTION

DISTRIBUTION AND INTEGRATION WITHIN THE BUILDING

Ductwork is the only mechanical system of a size sufficient to cause large scale alterations in other systems (Rush, 1986)

Because of the way this book is laid out you will have realized by now that in many buildings, particularly those that cannot be naturally ventilated or require air-conditioning, there is a definite need to allocate space for ducts that carry air. We know that these make the link between one of the major components of an environmental control system, the air handling unit, and the various zones in the building. The size of the ducts will vary, depending on what they are intended for and which system they are part of. They will be always larger than you want them to be, and if you are to ensure that they are not the cause of the alterations alluded to in the quotation it is as well to know something about their design.

AIR DISTRIBUTION SYSTEMS

With few exceptions air distribution systems follow one pattern, and that is one that is like a tree, a central trunk from which branches run out. If the system is part of an air-conditioning installation, or a heating and ventilating system, there will generally be two such distribution systems, one taking air to the various zones and another returning the air to the air handling unit. In most such cases the two ducts will be the same size and follow the same route through the building.

The exceptions to this standard pattern are systems that serve zones in which there is a need to discharge part of the air to outside for some reason, rather than return it to the air handling unit. In this case the two ducts would not be the same size and there would also be a secondary extract system. Another exception is where the structure or other part of the building forms part of the ventilation system. A raised floor may form a plenum chamber through which air flows before it enters the room, or a hollow column, or diaphragm wall may have air flowing through it; even a solar wall can be arranged to boost the temperature of the incoming outdoor air and carry it to the air handling unit. No matter how the distribution is arranged or what material it is made of, the important thing is to make the way as smooth as possible so that pressure needed to drive the air along is not greater than it need be. Air turbulence in the duct arising from abrupt changes in direction or local obstructions means more pressure must be developed by the fan, and that can produce noise and will certainly increase the consumption of electricity.

Ducts can be formed of various types of material: metal, concrete and reinforced plastic being amongst those in use; the most common, though, is galvanized sheet steel. When made of sheet steel the ducts are often rectangular in shape, although they may also be circular, and even an amalgam of both, with straight sides and rounded ends (referred to as 'flat oval'). Although a manufacturer will make any size that is paid for there is a range of preferred standard duct sizes produced by the Heating and Ventilating Contractors Association (HVCA DW/142).

When making allowance for space for any duct do not forget to provide for access and the thickness of any insulation. As a guide it is recommended that no less than 25 mm of insulation should be allowed, and for a rectangular duct having a width or diameter of 500 mm the side clearance should be 350 mm and the top and bottom clearance 200 mm (BSRIA, 1992b).

Obviously the size of the duct depends on the volume of air it is to carry. It is also a function of the velocity at which the air travels; the higher the velocity the greater the volume of air that may be carried and the smaller the duct. However, a higher velocity will create an increase in the resistance of the system to the flow of air, the resistance being related to the volume flow rate by a square power law. There is therefore a penalty to pay for the smaller ducts: it is the risk of noise, and the need for a more powerful fan to generate the pressure, which will cost more in terms of both capital and running costs. It is possible to obtain an approximate idea of the cross-sectional area of a duct, given the air volume and the allowable velocity from:

Air Volume (Q) m³/s = Velocity (V) m/s × Cross-Sectional Area (A) m², OR

$$A = Q/V$$

Typical recommended air velocities for low velocity, low pressure systems are:

Position in distribution system	Air velocity (m/s)
Main duct away from occupied zone	10
Branch duct, or close to quiet area	7 to 5
Entry into a grille, louvre or diffuser	Up to 4 (depending on noise level)

To give you some idea of what this means you should refer to the Design Exercise which follows this chapter.

The duct sizing diagram is based on this simple formula. However, designing a distribution system for 'real' involves much more than it used to, and you must realize that the guidance given by the diagram is only suitable for application at the strategic level of design.

There are three methods used to design ductwork systems, the most commonly used of which is that of 'Equal Pressure Drop'.

EQUAL PRESSURE DROP

In principle all ductwork is based on using the same pressure loss per metre length. The CIBSE design guide recommends that for a low velocity system a pressure drop of about 1 Pa/m run should be allowed and goes on to say that this method will produce higher velocities in the main duct, but as these are usually at some distance from noise-sensitive zones it should not cause a problem. Should you want to check the results given in the design project with the 'real' method then you need to refer to the CIBSE Guide (CIBSE, 1970, Section C-44). Note that if it is a high velocity system the allowed loss would be approximately 8 Pa/m run.

Just to add further to your growing technical vocabulary the other two methods are 'Constant Velocity' and 'Static Regain'.

CONSTANT VELOCITY

This is appropriate to air systems that are designed to carry solid materials such as wood waste. The aim is to ensure that there is a velocity in the ductwork that is sufficient to carry the waste, the velocity being determined by the type of material: for example dry wood waste would require a velocity of no less than 20 m/s.

STATIC REGAIN

This is most appropriate to the high velocity system and calls for a little more theory. It is based on the principle that a change in velocity causes an inverse change in pressure, and its main advantage is that its use produces a better balance in the system.

COMPONENTS

While the straight sections of the distribution system offer a resistance to the flow of air, it may be less significant than that produced by the changes in direction and section, especially in a complex building. Therefore, wherever possible bends should have generous radii, offsets should not be too acute and entries and exits not too abrupt.

In addition to these components there will also be the means of controlling the flow of air, commonly known as 'dampers'. These may operate automatically during an operation cycle to regulate the proportion of outdoor to recirculated air, or they may be set during the commissioning period so as to fine tune the balance of air flowing through the various sections of the installation. Others will be automatically controlled to adjust the outflow from the fan in the air handling unit. With the exception of the latter they are multi-leafed devices set in a flanged frame within the ductwork; the exception is more likely to be similar in operation to the iris of a camera.

AIR DISTRIBUTION IN A ROOM

Integrating the interior design of a room and the way air is distributed within it is too often a poor compromise, getting the aesthetics and the engineering together is not easy, and made worse because the principles of air movement are not always understood.

Let us first review what is expected of room air distribution. It needs to provide a feeling of freshness, there should be no stagnation and yet no one should complain of cold draughts. The temperature in the room should be at an acceptable level and even in value throughout the occupied zone (normally thought of as being the space between the floor and a height of about 2 metres). The maximum recommended temperature differential between head and feet is 1.5 degrees C. And finally, the means of doing all this must not cause a disagreeable noise, Table 8.1. The parameters of human comfort and warmth have already been reviewed, and we know something about the way in which the occupants of the room react to air movement; it should also be remembered that an air-conditioning system is designed to heat and cool a room.

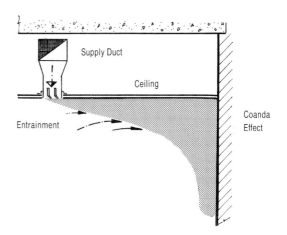

FIGURE 8.1 PATTERNS OF AIR DISTRIBUTION FUNDAMENTALS

Table 8.1. Maximum background noise levels

Typical Situation	Noise Level
Concert Hall, Recording Studio	NR 20
Theatre, Churches, Hotel Bedroom	NR 25
Cellular Office, Library	NR 30
Open Plan Office, Classroom	NR 35
Foyer, Restaurant	NR 40

It is recommended by the CIBSE that if stagnation of the air in a room is to be avoided its velocity should not be less than 0.1 m/s, and that the velocity at head level should be in the region of 0.1 m/s to 0.4 m/s, depending on the activity of the occupants and whether the system is heating or cooling.

Table 8.2. Maximum tolerable air velocities

Activity	Situation	Maximum Allowable Velocity (m/s) Heating	Cooling
Sedentary	Office	0.2	0.1
	Restaurant	0.3	0.15
Light work	Shops & light assembly	0.35	0.2
Medium work	Dancing	0.45	0.3
(After CIBSE, 1970, Section B, Table B3.1)			

Notice the difference in the allowable velocity between the heating regime and that of the cooling. An air-conditioning system will at some time switch from one regime to the other and could cause some discomfort in the process. It is best, therefore, to design to the most sensitive of the two rather than seek a compromise, and to take the cooling regime as the criterion.

THE PATTERN OF AIR MOVEMENT

The way in which the pattern of air movement develops in a room after it has left an outlet is to some extent dictated by natural laws. Obviously, if the incoming air is warm then it is buoyant and will tend to rise as it enters the room, and if it is cold then the reverse will hold true. However, some of the other controlling phenomena may not be as familiar:

Entrainment: as the stream of incoming air enters the room it entrains room air at its boundary; as a consequence of this the mass of moving air increases but suffers a reduction in velocity. This entrainment tends to set up a secondary circulation within the room, Fig. 8.1.

Coanda Effect: air, being a fluid, will associate itself with any surface it is brought into contact with. It will cling to it as it moves across it until some external force causes it to do otherwise. This is known as the Coanda Effect, Fig. 8.1.

Throw and Spread: the distance a jet of incoming air will move into a room is known as the 'throw'. The convention is that the throw is assumed to have terminated when the centre-line velocity is 0.25 m/s. After leaving the inlet point the jet will gradually diverge and spread to form a conical shape. Both the throw and the spread are a function of the shape of the air inlet and the velocity of the air as it leaves the inlet; they will also depend upon the proximity of any surfaces of the room. The dependence on geometry explains why the air inlets of a variable air volume system do not produce the optimum pattern of air movement when the cooling load is low and the air volume being delivered is correspondingly so.

Unfortunately there are other determinants that often have a strong effect on the pattern of air movement, and not all of these are under the control of the system designer. Localized sources of heat, such as those being emitted by computers, or the cold surface of a large window, can materially effect the movement of the entering air and be the cause of discomfort. Ceiling-mounted light fittings or exposed beams can deflect the air stream down on to the occupants.

When designing the layout of the air inlets care should be taken with their positions relative to each other and features of the interior design. For example, discomfort can result if two inlets are placed too close together: their respective air streams will collide and create localized increases in velocity. Similarly, placing an inlet close to a wall or partition can cause an effect that will be not unlike a waterfall of cold air.

Extract terminals do not need the same attention because, as was explained earlier, their domain of influence on the pattern of air movement is limited. They are most effectively placed close to where they are needed most. Putting them directly on the path of an incoming air stream is unwise, but otherwise the risk of short-circuiting the flow of the air supply is not high.

You will therefore realize that there is a need to integrate the interior design with that of the air delivery system, and now have a growing awareness of the interplay of the various determinants of the efficient functioning of an air-conditioning distribution system.

Air may be brought into a room in many ways and the position chosen for the inlets and outlets will not always be determined by a fundamental knowledge of air flow, but by the opportunities offered by the building design. There is a wealth of information on the subject, some of it highly theoretical, but there is also available much that is of a practical nature arising from direct observation and measurement. In many offices the ceiling void is most commonly used to conceal the ducts of an air-conditioning system and to make a direct connection with the air inlets and extraction points. Often the light fittings are designed to be an integral part of the extract point. In this way the heat generated by the lamp is removed at source and it is said that the cooling action increases the lamp's efficacy and life, Fig. 8.2. In the IT office the demand for space for telecommunication and electric power cables created the need for the raised floor. This provided the opportunity for using the space beneath the floor for the air ducts or even utilizing it as a plenum chamber. Making use of this opportunity to introduce cool air at floor level

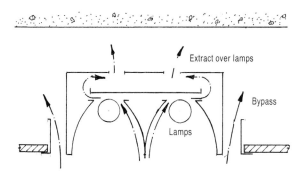

FIGURE 8.2 LUMINAIRE/EXTRACT AIR TERMINAL
(AFTER THORN LIGHTING TECHNICAL HANDBOOK, P. 158)

can cause discomfort; however the effect can be minimized by inducing a vortex in the air stream so that it speedily entrains room air, Fig. 8.3 (see also the Case Study of Briarcliffe House).

Avoiding the cause of discomfort and yet so arranging the air inlets that an effective pattern of air movement is produced is difficult, and never more so than when the occupants are to sit in one position for a considerable period of time. The design of an auditorium is a case in point; this is the subject of the Design Exercise that follows this chapter, but it is appropriate to review here some of the methods adopted for various well-known auditoria.

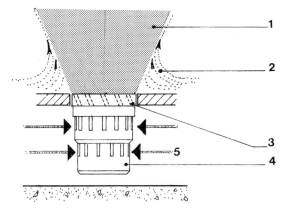

The Krantz System
1 Primary air vortex
2 Entrained room air
3 Air outlet giving swirl effect
4 Basket and air entry

FIGURE 8.3 SWIRL TYPE AIR INLET

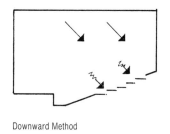

Downward Method

Upward Method

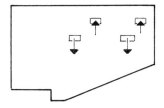

Side Entry

FIGURE 8.4 AUDITORIA, METHODS OF VENTILATION

Three methods are shown in outline in Fig. 8.4. Note that the area backstage must always be considered as a separate zone, and that any fly tower will have emergency smoke outlets or fans.

AIR MOVEMENT DOWNWARD

The air inlets are positioned at ceiling level and arranged so that the air moves towards the front of the audience. The position of the extract points is not too important, but may be placed in the risers of the aisle steps, towards the back of any balconies, especially where these are 'in the Gods', and even in the side walls. The inlets should not be above any banks of stage lights, otherwise the heat emitted by the lights will deflect the downflow pattern. This method allows the use of a wide difference in the temperature of the incoming to room air, and therefore may facilitate a lower air volume to meet a given cooling load. Fire Regulations will no doubt want the flow of the inlet fans to be reversible in the event of fire, or some other means of extracting the smoke made available. Theatres designed to use this method are: Royal Festival Hall, London; Derngate Centre, Northampton; de Doelan Concert Hall, Rotterdam.

AIR MOVEMENT UPWARD

This probably seems to be the most natural way to introduce air, but it does have some disadvantages as well as advantages. It is possible to provide a good coverage for a low noise level. However, if the air inlets are in the risers below the seats there is the possibility that the occupants will experience a draught, especially when the auditorium is being cooled and the air blowing over exposed ankles. This means that the temperature difference may not be as wide as that of the downward flow, and therefore, for a given cooling load the air volume must be higher, which in itself could cause a noise problem. A somewhat strange-looking, but none the less claimed to be effective, solution is to incorporate the air inlet in the backs of the seating. Theatres designed to use this method include the Berlin Philharmonic.

SIDE WALL WITH HIGH-LEVEL EXTRACT

By comparison with the two earlier methods this arrangement can facilitate ease of construction in that it is independent of both seating and the ceiling. It also offers a way of recovering the heat emitted by the audience and the lighting. Placing the input grilles below the level of the lighting may also be possible without bringing them too close to the audience; this would ensure that the pattern of air movement was not affected by the heat rising off the lighting. The method suits the present popularity being enjoyed by the displacement air method, for an example of which see the Case Study in Chapter Fourteen.

Both the Downward and Upward Flow methods are more suited to the larger auditorium where the audience are always facing the stage; the experimental theatre poses a quite different problem, though. This type of theatre demands that the position of the stage be capable of being changed. For some performances it may the orthodox proscenium arch, but for others it could be arranged for theatre in the round. If the ventilation system is to be designed so that it does not cause discomfort it must be arranged so that air is not blown down the audience's necks. One simple, but clever, solution to the problem was designed by Ove Arup & Partners for the Wilde Theatre, Bracknell. Their design is a modified downward flow system and consists of centrally placed inlets that terminate in movable turret heads. In this way the air may be aimed at the audience in most of the positions chosen.

AIR DISTRIBUTION DEVICES

There are several different types of air distribution devices, the most common being categorized as grilles, louvres or diffusers.

Grilles

The simplest form of grille is the stamped or perforated lattice. It is best to use these only for extract or air transfer points. The velocity through them should be kept low in the 1.5 to 3 m/s range, choosing the lowest for quiet situations. They may be obtained with a crude volume control device in the shape of a sliding perforated plate; in this form they are sometimes known as 'registers'.

Many fixed-bar grilles are available, but have a limited application, and it is advisable to use either the single or double deflection type with aerofoil vanes. These may be used for extract or air supply and provide directional control and can be fitted with a volume control damper. Face velocities in the range 2.5 to 6.0 m/s are typical. Noise will be generated by the cruder versions and they should not be used in quieter situations.

Diffusers

These come in various shapes, but principally linear, round (and half round), and rectangular. The linear variety are used for side wall, sill line and floor applications. It is possible to obtain them as a long continuous slot where the whole run is active, or to have only parts of the device active. They are best fitted with directional blades and, although it is possible to have control dampers fitted to them directly, this can produce an unacceptable noise level; it is far better to put such control in the branch duct. Ensuring an even flow across the whole length of a long diffuser requires care in the way in which the connection is made to the main duct.

Circular or rectangular diffusers are intended to be fitted in a ceiling, where they are designed to introduce large air volumes without draughts, the incoming air obeying the Coanda Effect, and for a large part clinging to the flat surface of the ceiling. Diffusers of this type may have either fixed or adjustable central cones and are designed to entrain room air so as to mix it with the incoming supply. Blanking pieces can be fitted within the diffuser to prevent downdraughts if the device must be fitted close to an obstruction.

DISPLACEMENT AIR METHOD

In rooms where a high air change rate is required without the possible disturbance caused by a consequential high air velocity, perforated ceilings have been used. They have been used in operating theatres, computer suites and also the clean rooms of some industrial processes.

An old and trusted method of introducing air in this way is to use textile socks. These are usually suspended from the ceiling and the open, permeable weave of the material forms thousands of very small air jets which, it is claimed, produce an evenly distributed temperature. Air change rates of 20 to 30 per hour are possible. The method has the advantage of being light in weight, and condensation will not occur on its outer surface. Once popular in industry, these have now gone up-market and may be obtained in a whole range of colours.

Introducing air into a room without giving it true direction and allowing it to displace room air is presently enjoying a certain popularity. The method is virtually the same as that previously used for operating theatres etc., as mentioned earlier. It involves introducing air, at temperatures only a few degrees above that of the room, through perforated

screens, often installed in free-standing columns, and allowing it to slowly spread across the floor in a Coanda Effect fashion. As the incoming air is warmed by the occupants and the heat emitted by the machines it moves upward, further displacing the room air until it stratifies above the occupied zone and is drawn into the extract system.

Swirl type air outlets have already been mentioned; these are proving to be far superior in operation by comparison with the other types of devices when they have been used in floor outlets. The advantage is principally due to the way in which the vortex of the incoming air entrains room air, and its incoming velocity decreases rapidly as the distance from the outlet increases.

INTEGRATION

Integration can mean the integration of services and structure in their function, or it can also mean the general coming together of the building systems in an efficient, planned manner. According to Richard Rush every building is integrated without the designers really being conscious of the fact. 'Integration results without intention because the criteria that serve as a basis for design are not specific to systems; they are specific to the buildings as a whole' (Rush, 1986). While this may be true it is sometimes less than obvious in many buildings. Effective integration needs the co-operation of the design team, and for their efforts to bear fruit their individual intentions require a conduit and an orchestrator; this role has been, and should be once again, that of the architect.

FUNCTIONAL INTEGRATION

Functional or physical integration can also take place in two quite different ways. It can be seen in the form of Kahn's 'servant spaces', the towers of the Richards Memorial Laboratories, and also those designed by Lloyd Wright for the Larkin Offices, where the construction is the container for the metal ducts that carry conditioned air; or more correctly, examples where the structural members or the fabric of the building have a dual role, being an essential part of the built form and a component of the building services system.

The duality of structure is not new; the Romans

used the raised floor and hollow walls to carry hot air to warm their homes and baths. It became one of the hallmarks of the Ove Arup Partnership, cruciform columns and double skin concrete shells being innovatively pressed into service to carry conditioned air in a variety of buildings, beginning with Arup's early collaborative work with the Architects' Co-Partnership and the design of the Brynmawr rubber factory.

One of the potential disadvantages of this duality springs from its lack of flexibility. The environmental control system is literally cast in concrete, and if there is a change in the use of the building it is virtually impossible to have the system respond to suit it. In these days, when every attempt is being made to keep down the use of electrical power, the resistance offered by concrete ducts is also a disadvantage, and the smoother metal duct will be preferred.

Despite this there is growing use of duality for some components of the building, but it may not be fully realized. I refer of course to passive solar design and in particular the use of solar walls in conjunction with mechanical ventilation and warm air heating, the Case Study of Briarcliffe House being a case in point. There is also a return to natural ventilation being brought about by towers. Reference has already been made to Waterhouse's Natural History Museum, London. Here outside air enters the building through terracotta grilles let into the wall below the basement windows and passes through canvas screens before being heated and travelling up flues built into the thickness of the wall to enter the galleries through registers at skirting level. Vitiated air is discharged through two tall towers, one of which has at its centre the flue from the boilers to enhance the stack effect (Olley and Wilson, 1985).

CONCEPTUAL INTEGRATION

We have already touched upon the need for integration, both in a general way (Chapter Four) and in particular with regard to the placing of air inlets in ceilings. The greatest problems can occur when the larger elements of the building services clash with the structural system; most usually this is when air ducts need to pass through structural plates or pass by structural members.

The depth of the horizontal services zone must be kept to a practical minimum, because space costs money and in a multi-storey building it can mean the loss of one storey height. There are various ways of doing this:

● By breaking the building down into several zones and serving each from its own vertical shaft. This implies a greater number of air handling units and an increase in the area of floor space dedicated to services. There are a number of building types that benefit from this approach, including residential blocks, hospitals and multi-tenanted offices; see Fig. 4.18.

● Utilizing a tartan grid for the structural system and planning the circulation so that the services may run in the ceiling space of corridors. Cross-overs in the ductwork could cause problems if the inlet and return ducts run in the same space. The structural system would not be acceptable for spaces that are to have a floor space unimpeded by columns.

● By exposing the ducts, either within the building or externally.

● By using a flat slab system where possible.

● By so arranging the structure that it is, in servicing terms, virtually transparent; see the Case Study of the Royal Life Building in Chapter Twelve.

● Adopting the functional integration concept, using the ducts as part of the fabric of the building; see the Case Studies in Chapters Thirteen and Fourteen.

SERVICE ZONES

The shape of a services shaft will determine how the ducts within may run when they move from a vertical to a horizontal plane; again the way in which the structure is arranged about the hole is important. Connections to equipment on the roof, or in the basement, can be made difficult and the services zones deeper without care being taken about the spatial relationship of plant room and shaft, Fig. 8.5.

The depth of the service zone depends on the complexity of the services and the structural system. Fig. 8.6 illustrates how a duct may be run in the depth of a concrete rib if it is continuous, but if the

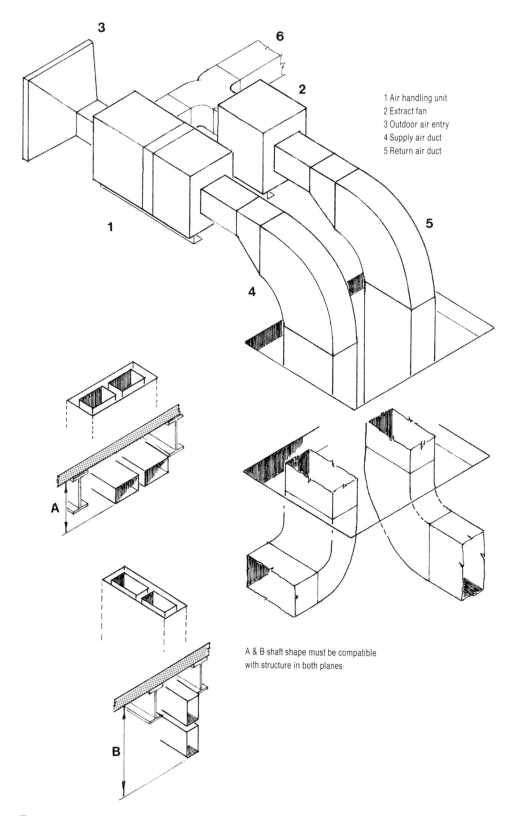

1 Air handling unit
2 Extract fan
3 Outdoor air entry
4 Supply air duct
5 Return air duct

A & B shaft shape must be compatible
with structure in both planes

FIGURE 8.5 INTEGRATION, SERVICE SHAFTS

structural system is a two-way waffle slab then the duct must lie below the rib. Various arrangements of service zones are possible; three are shown in Fig. 8.7, the most complex arrangement is that of Fig. 8.8.

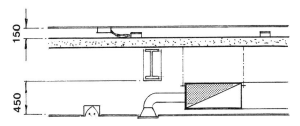

Low demand office: electrical supply below floor
Cable trunking: flat cable

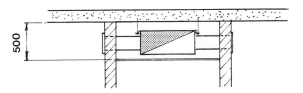

High demand office: raised floor carrying all services

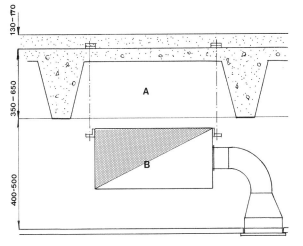

A: ducts can only run here if ribbed slab runs one way; branch ducts impossible
B: ducts here if structure is two-way waffle slab

FIGURE 8.6 INTEGRATION, AIR DUCTS & STRUCTURAL GRID

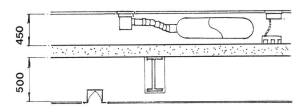

Residential: central duct serving rooms off a corridor

FIGURE 8.7 INTEGRATION, SERVICE ZONES

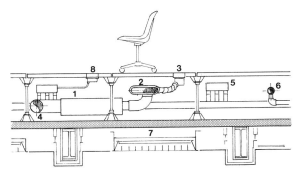

1 VAV unit or fan coil unit
2 Branch supply duct
3 Swirl type air inlet
4 Primary supply air duct
5 Electrical supply
6 Sprinkler supply
7 Luminaire
8 Electrical supply outlet

FIGURE 8.8 TYPICAL IT OFFICE WITH RAISED FLOOR

DESIGN EXERCISE ONE

A THREE-STOREY OFFICE

Let us now put into practice some of the techniques that have been outlined in the early chapters. Using them and the various space allowance diagrams we will determine the space needed for the building services of the modest three-storey office block shown in Fig. 9.1.

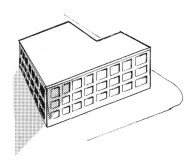

FIGURE 9.1 DESIGN EXERCISE ONE: THREE-STOREY OFFICE

THE CLIENT

The client is imagined to be a marketing organization and they have acquired a site on a business park. Their funds will not allow any special design and it must be assumed that the building will be typical of what is seen on such sites. There is one good feature and that is that the client wants to avoid using air-conditioning and would like as many naturally ventilated spaces as possible.

Many of the offices will be medium size cellular ones, with some one-person offices for senior staff,

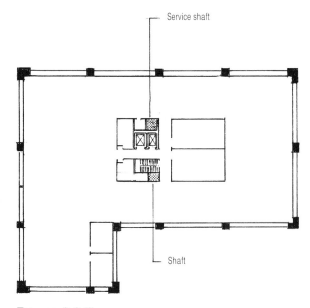

FIGURE 9.2 TYPICAL FLOOR PLAN

together with a meeting room on every floor and a space where the employees can take a break and have a coffee. The floor plan shown in Fig. 9.2 is to be taken as being typical. Looking at the floor plan you will notice that because of the plan depth it will not be possible to rely on natural ventilation throughout the building.

DESIGN STRATEGY

Because both the building and the way it is to be used are fairly simple there is no need for a complex environmental control system; there is a modest need for mechanical ventilation. Heat may be supplied by either radiators or natural convectors at sill level; these would have thermostatic control valves on them so that the occupants could be afforded a measure of control over the heat input. Using such simple units does have its disadvantages: they will inhibit any possible future re-arrangement of the offices and they can impose the same discipline on where furniture may be placed. This would have to be explained to the client. If complete flexibility is required then the spaces must be served either from the floor, which implies the use of a raised floor, or the ceiling. Next, the area that needs mechanical ventilation. This may be treated in one of two ways:

● It can be mechanically ventilated and heated by the same system, that is it would be independent of the general heating system.
● Or, it could be supplied with air to meet the needs of the occupants and be heated in the same way as the rest of the building.

The first option has the advantage that it can be designed to provide some flexibility in the arrangement of the inner zone, it being assumed that the space will be used partially as a service core and partially as a meeting space. The core would contain a lift, the staircase, toilets and a beverage dispenser or small kitchenette, Fig. 9.2. In summary then, the services system will need to provide:

● Cold water storage.
● Hot water.
● Heating.
● Mechanical ventilation plus heating.
● A lift.

There will be a need for a gas meter room, an electrical intake and distribution board, drainage and fire-fighting equipment.

ALLOCATION OF SPACE

Cold water storage
Assuming typical space/person for an office of 10 m², then number of occupants based on net floor area assumed to be 180.

Water storage required is 45 litres/person, total $= 45 \times 180 = 8100$ litres or 8.1 m³.

From BSRIA recommendation, space allowance with access space of 0.75 m all round is 20 m², clear height 2 m minimum.

Hot water storage
Allow 5 litres/person $= 5 \times 180 = 900$ litres.
Space allowance $= 4$ m², clear height 3 m.

Heating
Assuming that the building meets current Building Regulations, the glazed area is 70% and the air change rate is not greater than 2 per hour. Then the required boiler power, including standby, is 150 kW. Space Allocation 20 m².

Air handling plant
The area to be mechanically ventilated is 150 m² on each floor, total enclosed volume therefore: allow 5 air changes/hour. Air volume to be delivered $= 450 \times 5 = 2250$ m³/h or 0.625 m³/s.
A packaged air handling unit, placed on the roof, possibly sharing the same room as the water storage tank and the lift motor machinery, would provide this volume. It would have a heating coil within it coupled to the boiler to provide warm air. Space requirement 15 m².

Lift motor room and shaft
One lift would be provided mainly for use by disabled personnel, there being only three floors. The fitter occupants should be encouraged to use the stair; an attractively designed staircase would help.

Space Allocation: maximum number of passengers 5, lift motor room $= 7.5$ m², height 2.3 m, shaft dimensions approximately 1.5×2 m.

Electrical intake and meter room. Gas meter room
Although these two spaces would be quite separate their combined space requirement would be modest, allow a total of 10 m², height 2.5 m.

PLANT ROOMS AND SERVICES SHAFTS
The main components of the system are placed in two separate areas. Mention has already been made of the position of the cold water storage tank,

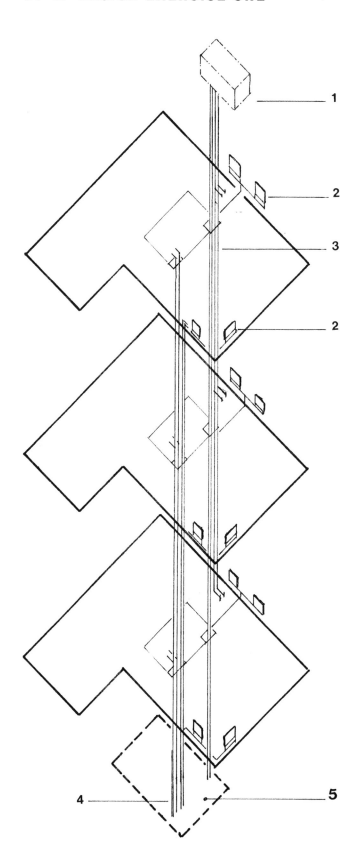

1 Air handling unit
2 Radiators
3 Service shaft: primary heating & air ducts
4 Service shaft: heating to radiators & hot and
  cold water
5 Basement plant room

FIGURE 9.3 DIAGRAM SHOWING MAIN
COMPONENTS OF SERVICES SYSTEMS AND
THEIR CONNECTIONS

the air handling plant and the lift motor machinery, these being placed on the roof. The boilers will be placed in a basement area to ensure that the roof is not overloaded.

Fig. 9.3 is a diagrammatic arrangement of the linkages between the main components and the terminal units.

Obviously there are other possible arrangements and you may like to consider them and compare them to this one. The next example is slightly more complex than this and includes air-conditioning.

CHAPTER TEN

DESIGN EXERCISE TWO

AN AUDITORIUM

This second design exercise concerns an auditorium, together with various ancillary rooms, to seat an audience of 800 people. It owes much to Professor Derek Poole, being an example he uses in his teaching. However it has been modified somewhat and any errors are therefore of my own making.

ACCOMMODATION SCHEDULE

Space	Area m²	Volume m³
Auditorium	650	12800
Foyer	800	2400
Box Office	20	50
Manager	12	30
Bar	40	125
Toilets	80	200
Cloakroom	80	200
Control Room	65	200
Technical Areas	30	90
Dressing Rooms		
Principals	48	120
Conductor	24	60
Others	170	410
Choir	132	330
Orchestra	120	300
Wardrobe	65	160
Rehearsal Room	400	1200
Green Room	200	560
Admin. Office	100	250
Total	3036 m²	19485 m³

The allocation of space for services is sometimes based on the total floor area, the rule of thumb for this being taken as 6 to 10%. For this particular case then the space requirement could be assumed to be about 182 to 304 m². However, although making this calculation may be of some comfort it is of little real use. It does not help to establish the size of the building's footprint, because the various items of the plant may be dispersed about the building; perhaps it is of some help during an early costing exercise. In my opinion it is a rule of thumb that belongs to the concept of the centralized plant room and is only suited when that is the case. A more informed approximation of the space needed may be obtained by considering the various larger items piece by piece. First, however, we need to decide on the type of environmental control system that will be needed.

ANALYSIS OF USE

It is assumed that the auditorium will be used for a wide range of performances and that, although there will be live theatre, there is no need for either scenery storage or a fly tower; this type of use is typical of the community theatres that were built during the 1980s. It is the policy to encourage the community to use these theatres for social activities as well as the more orthodox uses. There may therefore be exhibitions of work by the local arts society in the foyer and the bar will serve snacks throughout the day to encourage people to drop in and meet with friends.

One of the early tasks in the design process is to identify the various zones within the building (this technique was introduced earlier in Chapter Three) and from there identify the need for certain types of environmental control systems.

Space	Comment	Zone
Auditorium	Used only for performances, high occupation density over long period	One
Foyer Box Office Bar Toilets & Cloaks Offices	These will be in use whenever the building is open. Occupation mainly transitory	Two
Dressing Rooms	In use during rehearsals and performance	Three
Green Room Rehearsal	In use prior to a performance	Four
Technical Area & Wardrobe	Will need special treatment	Five

Considering each of these zones in turn:

Zone One: the auditorium is quite different in the way in which its need for environmental control changes over a short period; this arises from its function and the way in which the audience moves into and out of it. A typical cycle of the events looks like this:

Before a performance: winter.	Heat will be needed and a minimum rate of ventilation
Audience entering: winter.	Heat needed at first, but less as audience size increases and it may become self-sustaining. Ventilation rate proportional to audience size, outdoor air volume increasing.
Full house: summer.	Full outdoor air needed for ventilation if not air-conditioned.

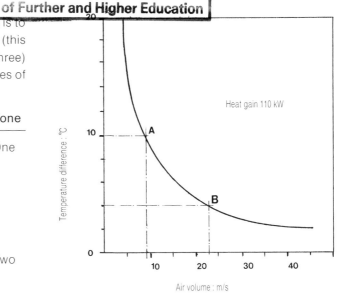

FIGURE 10.1 AIR VOLUME VERSUS TEMPERATURE RISE

For these reasons the auditorium should be treated as a totally separate zone. The question as to whether it should be air-conditioned or simply mechanically ventilated and heated would in reality be answered by a costing exercise, although you may also like to take the conceived public image of the place into consideration. If it is to rely on the cooling effect of outside air then there would be times, especially with a full house, when comfort could not be guaranteed.

For example: a full house of 800 people, plus the stage lights and solar gain, could generate a sensible heat gain of about 110 kW. In July the mean outdoor temperature in the south of England is 19 degrees C, this rises on average to 25 degrees by 1700 hrs before slowly cooling down again. If the temperature in the auditorium is to be kept at about 29 degrees C or below by introducing outside air at the mean value of 19 degrees, then the incoming air volume rate would need to be about 9 m³/s. However, should the incoming air temperature reach 25 degrees C then to maintain similar temperatures indoors the volume would need to be increased to 23 m³/s; see Fig. 10.1.

The conditions brought about by the worst scenario could be mitigated by drawing in air overnight and cooling the fabric of the building. However, to ensure that this would be effective the inner surfaces of the auditorium would need to be constructed so that there was sufficient exposed mass and that it would be cooled; the consequential hard surfaces may effect the acoustic quality of the auditorium. We will estimate how much space would be needed if the auditorium is to be air-conditioned and, as an alternative for comparison, if natural ventilation is to be relied on.

Zone Two

All the rooms in this zone may be naturally ventilated and heated. They are assumed to be in use throughout the day and until the building closes for the night. This occupation pattern is quite different to any of the other spaces and for this reason the heating system will be zone controlled. In planning the building this should be remembered and the rooms of the zone should be spatially related.

Zone Three

All the dressing rooms are selected for this zone. If the rooms have an outside wall then the normal reaction would be to have opening windows and to ventilate them naturally. However, this can pose a security problem because the rooms will be left unattended and may contain valuable personal property; open windows present an opportunity for even the most amateur thief, and nervous performers will no doubt forget to close them. Also, there will be toilets and perhaps showers adjacent to the rooms, and these are best mechanically ventilated. It may therefore be a good plan to mechanically ventilate and heat all the dressing rooms, or at least provide the necessary air change rate mechanically and supply heat by simple radiators.

Zone Four

The rehearsal and green rooms; these could be in use at the same time as the rooms of Zone Three. However, it is also possible that they may be in use when the rooms of that zone are not, and in this case they should be separately controlled. The type of system will depend on whether they can be naturally ventilated or not. Most companies prefer

rehearsal rooms to be daylit and naturally ventilated, and this preference should be worked towards and would argue against them being thought of as having the same requirements as the rooms in Zone Three. In this exercise it is assumed that both rooms will be naturally ventilated and heated simply.

Zone Five

Much depends on the type of work undertaken in the rooms. If there is to be any paint spraying then obviously there will be a need for a local mechanical extract system; woodworking machines have a similar need too. Wardrobes can be very stuffy and dank unless they are properly ventilated, and therefore a simple input and extract system should be installed.

Summary

Zone One:	Mechanical ventilation with warm air, or air-conditioning.
Zone Two:	Natural ventilation and a simple heating system.
Zone Three:	Mechanical ventilation and warm air.
Zone Four:	Natural ventilation and a simple heating system.
Zone Five:	Localized mechanical ventilation and simple heating, or a packaged warm air unit.

ALLOCATION OF SPACE

We can now proceed and allocate space for the major items of the various systems. Cold water will be required throughout the building, and in the UK there must be adequate storage facilities, and therefore we will start at this common need.

COLD WATER STORAGE

Water is stored so that there is provision to cover 24 hours of interruption of supply from the mains. The amount of water to be stored depends on how many people use the building and what they use it for. In a public building such as this it is difficult to decide on a reasonable criterion; it most certainly should not be the maximum seating capacity of the auditorium, but it needs to be more than the full-time paid staff.

On the assumption that the occupancy is equivalent to say 350 people, allow 45 litres per person (this is the same as that recommended by the CIBSE for 'offices with canteens'). And therefore on this basis:

$$\text{Storage volume} = 350 \times 45 \text{ litres}$$
$$= 15750 \text{ litres or } 15.75 \text{ m}^3$$

According to the Water Supply Bye-law 31, there shall be an unobstructed space above the tank for inspection purposes of at least 350 mm; if bolted-on tops are fitted this shall be increased to 500 mm. Sectional tanks shall be raised on supports to the extent that there is a minimum of 450 mm space underneath. In addition there should be access all round the tank, and for this a space of 0.75 m should be allowed.

If we use just one tank then it is suggested by BSRIA that the floor space (including the 1 metre allowance) for it must be no less than 15 m² for a tank 1 m high and that the overall height of the room should be no less than 2 m.

Summary:

Storage capacity	16 m³
Floor space	15 m²
Minimum height	2 m
Location	At highest point in the building, otherwise pressure pumping will be required.

HOT WATER STORAGE

Using the same assumption as that for cold water storage, the hot water storage should be:

5 litres/person

Storage capacity	$= 5 \times 350$
	$= 1750$ litres or 1.75 m³
Space requirement	25 m², including allowance for access
Minimum height	3 m
Location	Close to boiler that serves it, but it may be independently fired.

As a guide to the heat output required from the boiler plant assume a rule of thumb figure of 30 W/m³ of building volume. Obviously this allowance depends on the standard of insulation applied to the building and the exposed surface area; a compact, well-insulated building would need less heat than this. It also assumes that the layout is such that one central boiler plant is appropriate.

Heat output	19485 m³ × 30 =	585 kW
Plus stand-by allowance.	Total output =	900 kW
Space requirement, from diagram		= 80 m²
Height		4 m
Location	Roof: acceptable but check roof loading and noise intrusion. Ground floor: best location if access good, check need for flue. Basement: can be acceptable, access and ventilation important.	

AIR HANDLING PLANT

Only Zones One and Three are to be fully mechanically ventilated, the former may also be air-conditioned.

Zone One, Auditorium.

Case 1. Mechanical ventilation without ambient air cooling. (Fig. 10.1)
  A. Best case (ambient mean 19 degrees C, inside 29 degrees)
    Air volume required = 9.1 m³/s
  B. Worse case (ambient 25 degrees C, inside 29 degrees)
    Air volume required = 22.7 m³/s

Case 2. Air-conditioning
  Assume 12 litres/sec of air per person
  Air volume required = 800 × 12
    = 9.6 m³/s

This can be roughly checked to see if it would produce a difference in the temperature of the air in the room and the incoming air that would offset the sensible heat gain but not cause discomfort:

If sensible heat gain is 110 kW and air volume is 9.6 m³/s

then temperature difference $= 110/1.2 \times 9.6$

$= 9.55$ degrees C

and therefore if the indoor temperature is held to say 25 degrees C the incoming air temperature will be about 15.5 degrees, which is acceptable.

Space required for AHU

Case One A: (9.1 m³/s) = 60 m²

B: (22.7 m³/s) = 105 m²

Case Two: (9.6 m³/s) = 60 m²

Headroom required = 3.5 m

Location   Roof: preferred location. Above traffic pollution, and air inlet and discharge ducts can be short. Ground floor: Pollution at low level a possible problem. Basement: Access must be good. Long air inlet and discharge ducts most likely.

Note: care must be taken with the final position because of the noise generated by the unit, see layout diagram.

Zone Two, Dressing Rooms.

Assume 6 air changes per hour

Air volume required $= \dfrac{\text{Room volume} \times 6 \text{ ac/h}}{3600}$

$= \dfrac{1220 \times 6}{3600}$

$= 2.03$ m³/s

Space required for AHU = 20 m²

REFRIGERATION (WATER CHILLERS)

It has been determined that a supply air temperature of 15 degrees C would be acceptable, combined with a delivered air volume of 9.6 m³/s, the air-conditioning system being designed to hold the auditorium at 25 degrees C and 55% RH.

Using the psychrometric chart the difference in entropy ('total heat content') of the air in the auditorium and that of the incoming supply air is found to be 18 kJ/kg.

Therefore: cooling required = air volume ×

volumetric specific

heat content

× enthalpy

$= 9.6 \times 1.2 \times 18$

$= 207$ kW

This required output may be met by a packaged air cooled chiller, rather than a refrigeration set and a separate cooling tower. It could be placed on the roof as close to the air handling unit as is practical. It may be in the open so that heat may easily be discharged by the integral condenser heat exchanger. Noise can be a problem.

Space Allowance: 35 m² if in the open (allow at least 1.5 m all round for a satisfactory throughflow of air).

ELECTRICAL INTAKE & METER ROOM

A building of this size is not likely to need a substation, but there will need to be a space set aside for the incoming electrical supply, distribution board and meters. This space will require to be well ventilated and have a secure access to outside; a ground floor location is ideal.

Approximate demand:

General allowances for areas not air-conditioned (source BSRIA) 40 W/m²

$2386 \times 40 =$ 95 kW

Air-conditioning equipment (if applicable)

= 150 kW

Theatre lighting = 100 kW

Allowance for future development +25%

= 86 kW

Total = 431 kW   431/0.8 = 539 kVA

Space required: 24 m²: Height 3 m

GAS METER

The gas meter must be housed separately, and generally British Gas will require it to be as close to the boundary of the property as possible so that their responsibility for the connections is limited.

Space required: 4 m²; Height 2.5 m.

LIFT MACHINERY

At least one lift for the use of disabled people should be allowed for; ensure that this is adjacent to the foyer and the stairs.

Allowance for a light traffic electric traction lift, maximum number of passengers 5
Machine room dimensions (source: BSRIA):
7.5 m²; height 2.3 m
Shaft area approximately 4 m²

SUMMARY OF SPACE ALLOWANCE

Facility	Area m²
Cold Water Storage	15
Hot Water Storage	25
Boilers	80
Air Handling Unit Case 1A:	60
Case 1B:	105

Facility	Area
Air handling Unit Case 2:	60
Air Handling Unit, Dressing Rooms	20
Water Chiller	35
Electrical Intake	24
Gas Meter	4
Lift Machinery; Motor Room	7.5
Shaft	4

Total: Case 1A	239.5 No air-conditioning
Case 1B	284.5 No air-conditioning
Case 2	274.5 With air-conditioning

The area required for the services is in the range 8 to 9%, depending upon the decision whether to rely on ambient air to cool the auditorium or to install air-conditioning. Case 1A is the optimistic decision and carries with it the risk of discomfort due to overheating. It may be argued that if the climate is changing due to the loss of the ozone layer and hot weather is to be the norm during the lifetime of the building then it is an unwise choice. Case 1B is more realistic but demands a greater throughflow of air and therefore a more powerful air handling unit and larger distribution ducts; the demands for electricity to drive the fan will also be higher. Case 2 is, of course, the air-conditioning system. It offers improved control throughout the year, but constitutes a greater threat to the environment.

POSITIONING THE EQUIPMENT

Figures 10.2 and 10.3 show various options for the position of the main items of the services system, then also explore the classical ways in which air is introduced into and extracted from an auditorium.

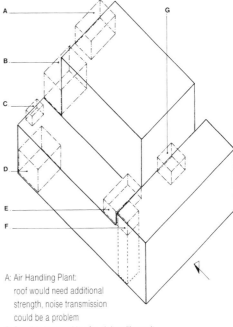

A: Air Handling Plant:
roof would need additional strength, noise transmission could be a problem
B: Possible best position for air handling unit
C: Cooling tower
D: Boiler room, adjacent electric and gas meters
E: Alternative second boiler room and cold water storage tank- check height against that of any first floor toilets
F: Lift shaft, possibly hydraulic action
G: Cold water storage tank, alternative position

FIGURE 10.2 POSSIBLE POSITIONS OF EQUIPMENT

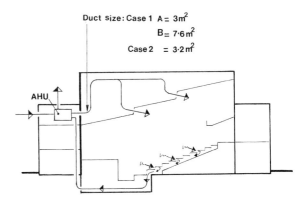

FIGURE 10.3 CHOSEN VENTILATION SYSTEM

CHAPTER ELEVEN

CASE STUDY: CRANFIELD LIBRARY

INTRODUCTION

Cranfield Institute of Technology is a university that specializes in post-graduate studies and continuing professional development in applied sciences, engineering, energy management, manufacturing and management. The new library, opened in October 1993, was designed by Sir Norman Foster and Partners and brings together a collection of books that was previously held in five different places scattered across the site. It forms a focus for the Institute and is designed not solely as a library but also as a meeting place at the heart of the campus.

Claimed to be the 'library of the future', it is designed to meet the needs of the students of today, providing them with books and a place in which to study, and to be adaptable to the changes in the way libraries will be used in the foreseeable future. An IT centre on the ground floor is linked to the campus computer system, and this serves a network of 300 peripheral points throughout the library. This may be logged on to at access points on the carrells so that the library users can have access to campus data banks or use applications, and to log into remote, off-site networks such as the Joint Academic Network (JANET). The Library envisages growth in the use of the system and an increase in the number of PCs and CD-ROM readers as more and more information is transferred from books to disk, Fig. 11.1.

FIGURE 11.1 THE LIBRARY, GENERAL VIEW

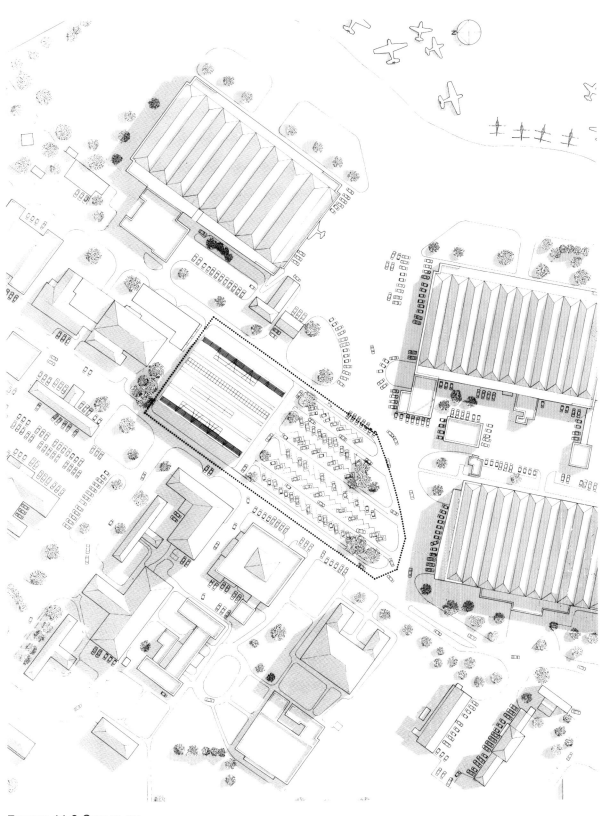

FIGURE 11.2 SITE PLAN

DESCRIPTION

The building has a simple but elegant appearance with four barrel-vaulted roofs supported by a fair-faced concrete frame covering a three-storey square plan that has a total floor area of 3000 m². The front elevation and two sides of the building are completely glazed by a curtain wall of glass that has a selective coating, while the rear wall covering the service zone is louvred in a similar fashion to the

Stockley Park building (AJ, 1989) also by Fosters. The outer vault of the roof arches over the edges of the building proper at both the front and the sides so that a canopy is formed over the entrance and covered walkways are produced along each side. Protection from solar gain and sky glare is provided by a louvred out-rigger that forms part of the structure beneath the edge of the roof vault. The overall effect is that of a sheltered cloister down

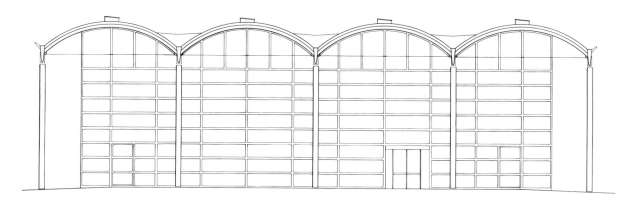

FIGURE 11.3 FRONT ELEVATION

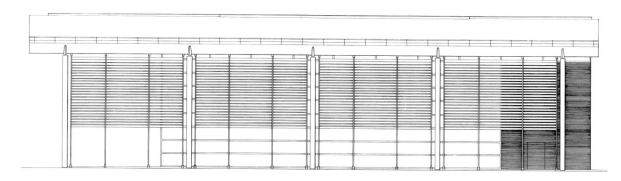

FIGURE 11.4 SIDE ELEVATION

both sides of the building and a 'forum' at its entrance; Rome in a hi-tech toga has come to Cranfield, Figs 11.2 & 11.3.

Daylight floods into the building at its edges through the floor-to-ceiling windows, diffused at times by the louvred screens, and it is brought into the centre of the building through long lights cut through the top of the vaulted roof. Beneath each roof light is a gull's-wing baffle; designed to improve the distribution of light not unlike those used by Kahn in the Kimball Art Museum in Austin, Texas, who referred to them as a 'modifier of the light' (Rush, 1986, p. 64), Figs 11.4–11.6.

The square plan is cut into by a centrally placed 'atrium' that makes a direct connection with the entrance, providing an open space for socializing and drinking coffee on the ground floor that rises clear through the vaults of the roof above. Rising

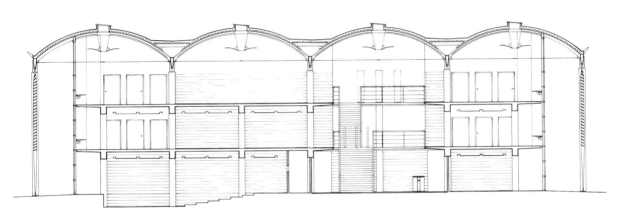

FIGURE 11.5 CROSS-SECTION

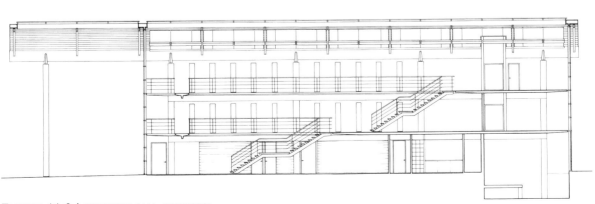

FIGURE 11.6 LONGITUDINAL SECTION

through the atrium is a glass-treaded staircase that links all three floors. The mannered elegance of this entrance into the library is unlike any other modern university and most certainly speaks not of a cloistered calm but of a hi-tech pursuit of knowledge. On the ground floor there is a state of the art lecture theatre capable of seating 180, three seminar rooms, two of which seat 30 and one that seats twice that number, a library area, a space for archives, a building services plant room and the open area of the coffee bar, Fig. 11.7.

The two upper floors are presently more particu-larly dedicated to the conventional function of a library with the usual book stacks and sources of reference, together with offices and workrooms. Unlike other libraries the study carrells on both of these floors are on a simple continuous bench that is supported off the curtain wall. This runs the whole length of the perimeter without interruption or the usual low screens separating one reader from another. A further difference, and it is of course the singular one that lays claim to this being the 'library of the future', is the inclusion of PCs on the carrell bench, Figs 11.8 & 11.9.

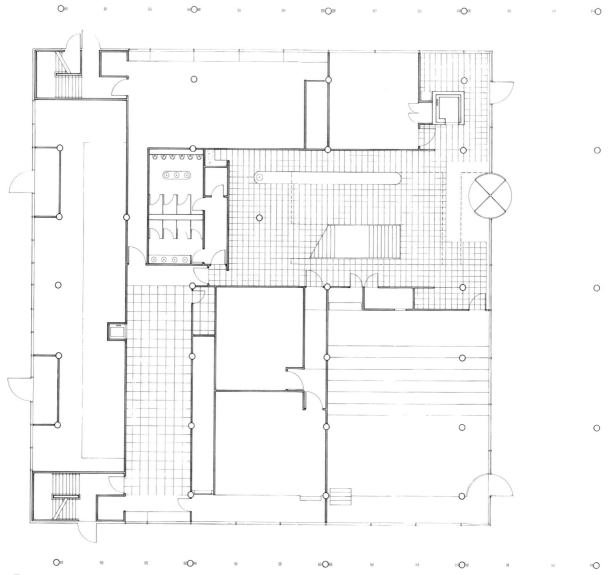

FIGURE 11.7 GROUND FLOOR PLAN

BUILDING SERVICES

ENVIRONMENT

There are several environmental control zones in the building, the largest one being that of the main bookshelf area. Here the zone is mechanically ventilated and heated by warm air during the winter. In the warmer months the preferred energy conserving regime is to limit the maximum internal temperature to 26 degrees C by introducing ambient outside air without any mechanical cooling. Should it prove sometime in the future, as the use of PCs increases,

that it is not possible to keep within this maximum temperature, then the cooling system which is already available will be brought on line.

The archives on the ground floor are in a separate zone that is fully air-conditioned by its own completely separate system on a 24-hour schedule to ensure a stable environment throughout the year, and in particular to maintain control over humidity so as to prevent damage by mildew. Humidity control (50% +) is necessary for the conservation of books and other printed material, and this requires cooling plant, plus efficient filtration and a

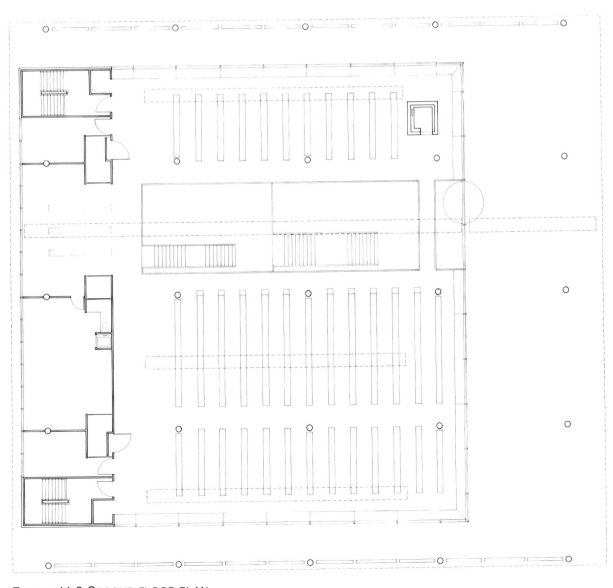

FIGURE 11.8 SECOND FLOOR PLAN

slightly cooler temperature (20 degrees C) than would be acceptable elsewhere.

Another individual zone is the lecture theatre where comfort cooling is provided. Each of the three seminar rooms is treated as a separate zone and provided with mechanical ventilation. This separation of the zones, even down to making individual zones of the smallest seminar room, not only ensures that they are only serviced when in use and that the individual system efficiently responds to that use, it also facilitates the costing of their use, this being part of the policy of designing the library so that it may be used for conferences and costed accordingly, Fig. 11.10.

CENTRAL PLANT ROOM

The compact, square plan form of the building lends itself to a central plant room, unlike a long, linear plan or a scattered number of buildings linked by a common circulation corridor where several zone-related rooms would be appropriate. All the main components of the environmental control system are grouped together in a plant room on the ground floor that runs the full length of the rear of the building. This facilitates maintenance and the future need to replace some items, services tending to have a shorter life than the building they serve; it also limits the need to run pipes carrying water into areas where there is a risk of serious damage should one leak.

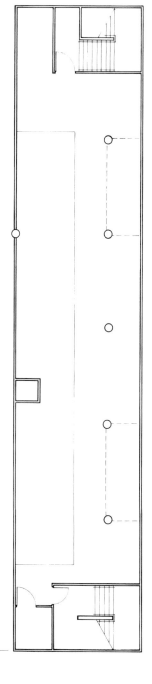

FIGURE 11.9 LOWER GROUND FLOOR PLAN

The louvred back wall of the building incorporates air intake louvres; these are situated at either end of the wall, and an air discharge louvred section is in the centre, well away from the intake points. Plant Room Area 200 m²; Vertical Risers, Total Area 40 m²; Building Area 3000 m².

AIR HANDLING UNITS

Each zone is served by an individual air handling unit. The units that serve the three larger zones are installed within the plant room, while the smaller units that are connected to the other zones are sited within the zone. The output of the air handling units is given in Table 11.1.

Table 11.1. Air handling units

Zone Served	Output (m³/s)	Approx Size L × W × H (m)
Main Bookshelf Area	9.85	9.0 × 2.2 × 2.0
Archive Area	2.60	3.2 × 1.2 × 2.20*
Main Lecture Theatre	3.00	3.8 × 1.6 × 1.4
Large Classroom	1.00	5.0 × 0.7 × 1.0
Small Classroom 1	0.50	3.0 × 0.7 × 1.4*
Small Classroom 2	0.5	3.0 × 0.7 × 1.4*

NB: Units indicated thus: *are double-height models. (Courtesy of J. Roger Preston & Partners.)

COOLING SYSTEM & LOW TEMPERATURE HOT WATER SUPPLY

Cooling is provided to the air handling units by direct expansion (DX) refrigeration units (refer to Chapter Four for a description). The low temperature hot water for the heating coils in the units is supplied not by boilers in this instance but by step-down heat exchangers fed with steam from the campus distribution system. Note that this is now an uncommon arrangement and most probably exists because the campus was at one time designed for and maintained by a Government department and, like many other such sites, has a central installation of steam-generating boilers.

AIR DISTRIBUTION

The conditioned air for the Main Library leaves the plant room in a duct that rises up the vertical shaft shown on the diagram and enters a space within the valley of the roof vaults. Here the duct travels horizontally to feed linear air diffusers that are integrated with the edge of the domed ceiling. Air is extracted at high level through louvres that run alongside the fluorescent lamps and returns down the vertical shafts to the plant room, Fig. 11.10.

In general the lecture theatre and the smaller classrooms are treated similarly. Air is introduced through linear diffusers that provide the edge to the suspended ceiling, and is extracted back through the void above the ceiling.

The exception is the arrangement for the Archives, where the conditioned air is brought directly into the book storage space within a raised floor, and introduced through perforations in the floor (the displacement air method described in Chapter Eight) and subsequently taken out at high level.

ELECTRICAL SUPPLY

Electrical power is supplied from the campus low voltage system. This enters into a distribution centre in the plant room area and is fed to each floor level, where there are two small power and lighting distribution boards.

CONCLUSION

This new building for Cranfield Institute fulfils a long-felt want; students say that it is a joy to work in – especially after the run-down accommodation that preceded it. It is designed to be the 'heart' of the campus and focal point of social togetherness as well as a library. Only time and use will tell whether these identities are compatible.

It is doubtful whether any of the design team would claim that the building is an exemplar of the energy conscious building. The building has a compact form, the wall to floor ratio is 3.71:1; it is most often flooded with daylight, the glass used has a selective coating to improve its equivalent thermal transmittance, but even so it is largely a glass box – an elegant one of course. Despite the preferred environmental strategy for the Main Library area, using only the cooling effect of the ambient air, it is an air-conditioned building and it needs to be so. The building services have been well thought out, the whole volume is treated as a number of separate zones and controlled as such to produce effective

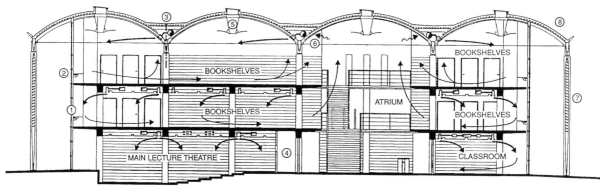

1 Typical Carrell position with integral power, data and voice distribution
2 Low 'E' fully glazed façade
3 Siphonic roof drainage system
4 Projection room

5 Specially designed uplighting system combined with rooflights, diffusers and reflectors
6 Integrated second floor supply and extract system
7 Louvred solar shading
8 Overhanging solar shading canopy

FIGURE 11.10 BUILDING SERVICES, CROSS-SECTION SHOWING AIR DISTRIBUTION

and efficient operation. However, the design is carefully understated and, using known technology, is there simply to serve the building rather than to advance new ideas.

It is a deceptively simple-looking building, which is of course one of the hallmarks of Sir Norman Foster and Partners' designs, but it is the product of careful analysis of the client's brief and one that is adaptable to the needs of the 'library of the future'. The design of the building services echoes that

methodology and is no more complex than it needs to be. At the moment its elegant simplicity stands in stark contrast to the sheds that are its neighbours; there is a crude simplicity born of austerity rather than a rigorous synthesis and application of Modernist principles.

Architects: Sir Norman Foster and Partners
M. & E. Engineer: J Roger Preston and Partners
Structural Engineers: Ove Arup and Partners

CHAPTER TWELVE

CASE STUDY: ROYAL LIFE OFFICES

INTRODUCTION

This office building for 1000 people was designed by Arup Associates and opened in July 1991. It accommodates the various divisions of Royal Life Insurance that were previously in offices scattered around Peterborough, Cambridgeshire. Its multi-discipline design team was faced with three challenges: 'to respond sensitively to the landscape of a rural site; to create a building form which provides flexible office areas; and to integrate the structure and servicing systems of the building for maximum environmental benefit' (Arup Associates, 1991).

The building sits on a site above the River Nene in what is still largely a rural site, although it has a neighbouring business park development and, more recently, within sight of it the large headquarters office of Pearl Assurance. There are 10600 m² of net office space, together with a computer suite of 1200 m², staff dining facilities, and a multipurpose sports hall.

In responding to the challenge posed by the site and the client's wish that all the offices should have a similar outlook, the design team developed the concept of a linear form. Orientating this form towards the already mature belt of trees to the north of the site provided several benefits: it gave the occupants some visual relief from working with VDUs; it turned the office area away from the road that borders the site and the traffic noise inevitably accompanying it, and it reduced the risk of uncontrolled direct sunshine which can be a major problem in a modern office.

Uncontrolled direct sunshine can make the reading of VDU screens difficult because of the glare it causes on them, and combined with heat emission from the machines in the office it can give rise to an undesirable increase in the cooling load. Rather than reduce the problem by either using solar control glass, which reduces daylight and increases the use of electric lighting, or louvred screens that would deny the occupants the outlook desired by the client, it was decided to turn the major glazed elevation of the offices away from the sun. However, the occupants benefit from the sun where its presence is welcome – social spaces such as the dining room and its terrace face the south.

The client's brief identified two main functional areas: the offices and the facilities that support them. The requirements of these two areas divided equally simply: open plan spaces with a few cellular closed spaces within them, and these to be given the desired contact with outside, and more enclosed spaces for the support facilities with little dependence on outlook.

DESCRIPTION

These determinants of site and function, together with those of access to the site and the building, largely formed the linear shape of the building and its position. To the south is the entrance to the building, slightly off-centre and clearly marked by a glass screen that shields the entrance and provides access to a terrace that is at a lower level and

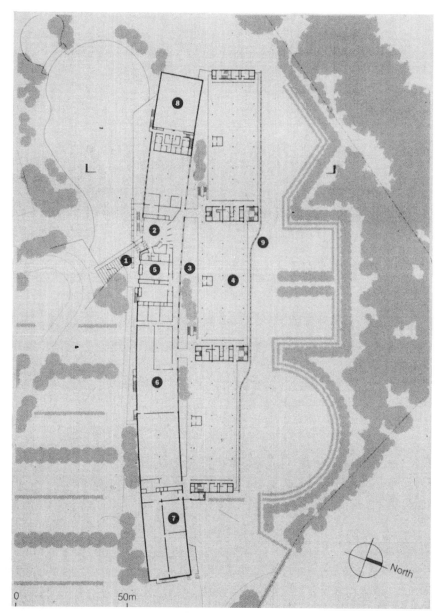

Key:
1 Main entrance
2 Reception
3 Internal street
4 Office areas
5 Conference room
6 Computer suite
7 Central plantrooms
8 Sports hall
9 Glazed screen wall

FIGURE 12.1 LEVEL 2 PLAN

overlooks an ornamental lake. This southern elevation fronts the curved block that contains the dining room and the support facilities, thus forming a buffer zone to limit the entry of direct sunshine into the offices beyond. This connects to and contrasts with the more rectangular plan areas of the offices to the north. Bridging between the two, and providing a link in both the concrete and corporate sense, is the street: an enjoyable internal space that combines aesthetic value with the practical, being circulation space and a social space of varying shape lit with shafts of sunlight coming through the clerestory above, Figs 12.1 & 12.2.

THE OFFICES

There are three floors of office accommodation, mainly of open plan spaces with a few closed offices for senior personnel and meeting rooms. These lie between the street and a circulation space that stands back from the glazed wall on the northern

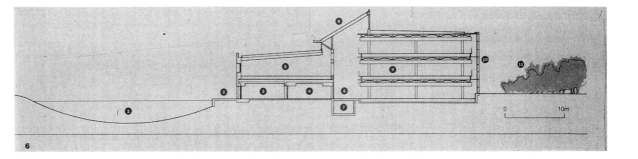

Key:

1 Lake
2 Dining terrace
3 Dining room
4 Coffee lounge
5 Support facilities
6 Internal street

7 Service tunnel
8 Street roof
9 Office areas
10 Glazed screen wall
11 Formal gardens

FIGURE 12.2 CROSS-SECTION

elevation. Planning of the office layout is strongly related to a structural grid of major and minor bays, the former providing for the open plan spaces while the latter offer provision for the cellular offices, Fig. 12.3. The treatment of the ceiling varies with the size of the bay; those of the minor bays have a conventional flat ceiling that gives access to the services above it and is suited to the possible arrangement of the partitions for the cellular office. Over the open plan spaces of the major bays the ceiling is a suspended white metal vaulted panel that serves to reflect the light from the luminaires suspended below, and also to conceal the return air duct and to carry the sprinkler heads. The whole of the floor of the office area is raised 600 mm to provide space for services and act as a plenum for the incoming conditioned air.

On the northern elevation there is a glazed screen wall; 180 m long and 12 m high, it sweeps along the whole of the elevation, curving around the steps formed by the staircase towers. It does not connect with the edge of the floors to the offices, for it stands back from the edge of the frame of the building – a transparent plane between the inside and the landscape outside. Cool north light comes in through the screen and penetrates deep into the offices, the penetration only being reduced by the height of the edge beam below the floor slab. Within

FIGURE 12.3 TYPICAL OFFICE

the screen there are openable lights which are intended to be operated by the office workers to provide them with some partial control of the internal environment, Fig. 12.4.

BUILDING SERVICES

ENVIRONMENT

There are several environmental control zones in the building, the most critical of which is considered to be the Computer Suite, and it is this which takes precedence over all else in so far as the services design and operation are concerned. The offices are only provided with cooling if it is not needed by the Computer Suite. However, as there is surplus capacity in the chillers, a measure of cooling will usually be available for them.

The largest zone is the office area, which is sub-divided into three, each division having its own air handling unit on the roof above the service core. In addition there are the Dining Room, Coffee Lounge, Kitchen and the Sports Hall.

CENTRAL PLANT ROOM

In this linear plan form building the main plant room, or more accurately the energy centre, is placed away from the noise-sensitive area and adjacent to the service access road and unloading bay. The tunnel carrying the distribution system of pipes and cables, running as it does below the street, echoes the main circulation route of the building; it links the energy centre with the vertical service cores and the air handling units that are above them.

The arrangement for the supply of heat and power does not follow the orthodoxy of boilers and sub-station, instead it springs from the need to provide a clean, dependable supply of power to the computers at an economic level. Three gas fuelled co-generation sets, each having an electrical power output of 276 kW, are at the heart of the installation; these supply both heat and power to the whole building. During cold weather the heat that is needed is supplied by these gas fired engines, and at the same time the power they generate is supplied in parallel with Eastern Electricity's supply to reduce consumption below the maximum demand figure.

Should there be a failure in the mains supply all the generation sets are brought on line to ensure that power is supplied automatically to essential demand points across the site.

The arrangement has the advantages of co-generation, in that it provides a stand-by facility to give power to essential users, it generates electricity efficiently and supplies heat to the building. The system relies on the balanced utilization of both heat and power, and this is ensured when heat is needed but the demand for power is low by the use of a thermal storage vessel. Water in this store is then heated by immersion heaters that are powered by the surplus electrical supply. Should heat not be required when there is a demand for stand-by generation, then the surplus heat is dumped through river water-cooled heat exchangers.

COOLING SYSTEM

In addition to optimizing the efficiency of the co-generators, the generation of cooling capacity is arranged to use as much 'free' energy as possible. To this end the chillers that supply chilled water to the computer room coolers and the air handling units for the offices receive their cooling water from the adjacent River Nene when its water temperature is lower than that of the cooling towers. River water is also used, after treatment, directly through the pre-cooling coils of the computer coolers. Mention has already been made of the priority for cooling that is given to the computers. However, there are three chillers installed, each one capable of carrying 60% of the computer cooling load and there-fore, unless there is an unprecedented high heat gain in the Computer Suite or a failure in a chiller, there will be sufficient surplus capacity to meet the needs of the offices.

AIR HANDLING UNITS

The three office zones are served by four air handling units located at roof level. Two of the units are rated to deliver 9 m³/s and two are at 18 m³/s. The air from the unit is ducted down through the service core to split and serve the space on either side of the core as far as a cavity barrier within the raised floor. The raised floor to the offices acts as a plenum and carries the air to the entry point of swirl

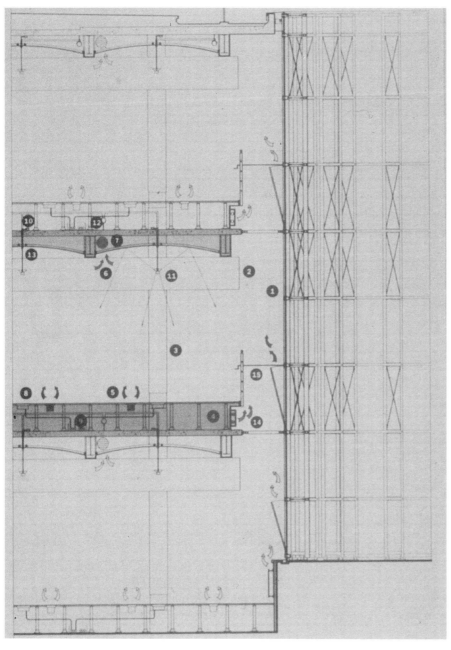

Key:
1 Glazed screen wall
2 Concrete beams
3 Concrete columns
4 Raised foor air plenum
5 Twist air outlet
6 Return air through ceiling
7 Return air duct in minor bay
8 Electrical floor outlet
9 Power/voice/data supply
10 Lighting power supply
11 Fluorescent up/down light
12 Sprinkler main
13 Sprinkler head
14 Perimeter heating
15 Manually opening window

FIGURE 12.4 CROSS-SECTION ADJACENT TO GLAZED SCREEN WALL

type outlets set at regular intervals in the floor. The conditioned air entrains and mixes with the ambient room air before leaving the occupied zone and drifting upward to be extracted at ceiling level and returned via the core to the air handling unit for re-use or discharge to outside. Apart from the usual heating and cooling coils, the air handling units also have incorporated a run-around coil that takes heat out of the vitiated air before it is discharged outside.

In an effort to reduce the discomfort felt from any cold downdraughts that may be developed by the glass screen north wall perimeter, convector heaters are fitted at the edge of the floor plates on

Key:
1 Glazed screen wall
2 Concrete beams
3 Concrete columns
4 Raised floor air plenum
5 Twist air outlets
6 Return air into minor bay
7 Return air through light fittings
8 Return air duct
9 Electrical floor outlet
10 Power/voice/data supply
11 Lighting power supply
12 Lighting control gear
13 Fluorescent up/down light
14 Sprinkler range pipe
15 Sprinkler head

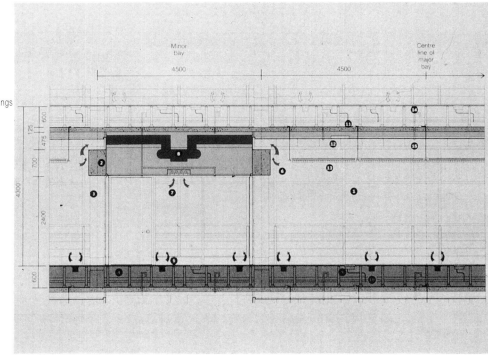

FIGURE 12.5 INTEGRATION OF STRUCTURE AND SERVICES

floors two and three, and at the bottom of the screen on the ground floor.

INTEGRATION

Arups have honed the development of the spatial framework of the buildings they design, and this building is an example of the art, with the rhythm of the major–minor bays. The structural system of secondary beams above primary beams, combined with a raised floor acting as both plenum and distributor of cabling, facilitates the integration of services and is, as the design team claim, 'virtually transparent to all horizontal service distributions', Fig. 12.5.

ELECTRICAL SUPPLY

An uninterruptible power supply system provides a continuous clean supply to the Computer Suite; this is capable of running completely independent of the co-generation installation. Power is distributed from a low voltage switch room to the other parts of the building along the tunnel below the street in an encapsulated busbar system, the encapsulation being made necessary by the need for sprinkler fire protection within the tunnel. The supply rises up the service core to distribution boards at each floor.

CONCLUSION

The form of this building is a good example of how an enlightened ordering of the problems set by the site and the brief may inform the design. Integration of services and building is typical of Arup Associates and now has become expected of them; nevertheless it has to be admired and seen as an example worth learning from.

In their pragmatic analysis of the problems that uncontrolled direct sunlight may cause in a modern office the designers have rejected the methodology of passive solar design, seeing, in this instance, sunshine as being more a nuisance than a benefit. However, in doing so they have reduced the inevitable demand for cooling in such an office and therefore indirectly saved energy. This ordering of the problem is quite different to that which the same practice used on the case that follows.

Architects, Engineers & Quantity Surveyors: Arup Associates

CHAPTER THIRTEEN

CASE STUDY: BRIARCLIFF HOUSE

INTRODUCTION

This office building was designed by Arup Associates for the Leslie Godwin Group, who required a high quality building for the speculative market. It contains 8250 m² of office space on virtually four floors over and at the front of an existing shopping mall, the latter not being of the highest quality. Since its opening the building has won the Office of the Year Award and a Civic Trust Award.

The building sits on a U-shaped site that is on the fringe of Farnborough, Hampshire. Two thirds of the perimeter of the site is bordered by busy roads,

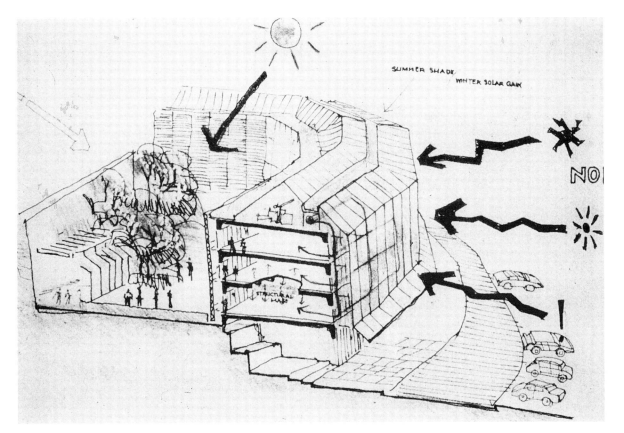

FIGURE 13.1 EVALUATION OF PROBLEMS AND CONCEPTUAL SKETCH

one being a four-lane highway serving the town, a car park and a bus route; the remainder is shared with the Kingsmead Shopping Centre. Farnborough and the air show are of course synonymous, and therefore the noise of aircraft flying low over the area is added from time to time to that of vehicular noise. Also, most of the perimeter faces southward and the elevation of the building receives solar gain for much of the day, Fig. 13.1.

The client's brief was to design a building that would provide a new and attractive front entrance to the existing shopping mall. It was to incorporate office space that would provide flexibility in the arrangement of enclosed and open plan offices and these were to be planned so that the floor areas could be subdivided into 600 m² and 850 m² separate lots so that they would be suitable for a multi-tenanted arrangement.

DESCRIPTION

Arup's response to the problems posed by the site and its environment was to turn them to good effect and produce a building that in action denies the first impression it gives of being simply another all-glass office block.

In response to the present problem of noise and the possible nuisance that excessive solar gain may cause, they produced a deep buffer space in the shape of a wrap-around wall that is a fly sheet over the southward U-shaped elevation of the building. The 'fly sheet' is 3300 m² of Pilkington's tinted Amourplate planar structural glazing system that stands about 1 m away from the reinforced concrete frame of the building. Unlike the sinuous continuous curve of the curtain wall of the Willis Faber Dumas building in Ipswich, this one is faceted. It starts above ground as a canopy above the heads of the passing shoppers and rises to cover the whole elevation from there to above roof level, where it forms space for the plant room. The way in which this integrates with the environmental control system will be described shortly, Figs 13.2–6.

Lying at the back of the curtain wall is the U-shaped office block. Constructed of reinforced concrete, it is a framed structure of perimeter ring beams supported on circular columns with deep

FIGURE 13.2 GENERAL VIEW OF BUILDING

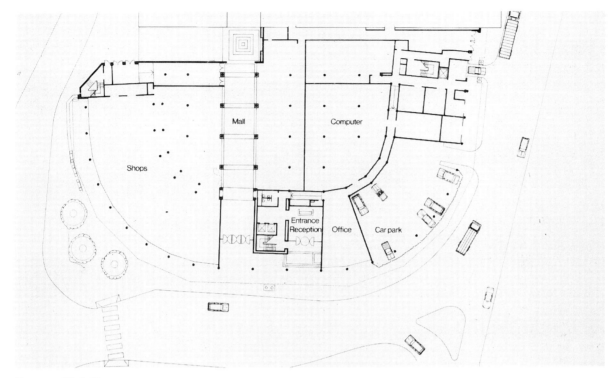

FIGURE 13.3 GROUND FLOOR PLAN

concrete ribs spanning 14.4 m between the beams. The elevation facing into the buffer zone is a mixture of single-glazed units and insulated panels which may be interchanged to suit changes in office layout. On the outside face are electrically driven, automatically controlled louvres. Providing an out-look and visual relief for the building's occupants is a glazed wall that looks out on to a courtyard that is within the inner curve of the U. Bridging across the legs of the main building is a staff restaurant, coffee lounge, bar and the kitchen. Entry into the offices is at ground floor level; the Reception Area and the Computer Suite are the only spaces occupied by the Leslie Godwin Group, the remainder, retail outlets that front the elevation at street level.

Inside the offices the ribs of the main beams are exposed and fan out radially from the front eleva-tion, breaking down the long view of the open plan areas. The articulation of this structure changes as the beams meet with the circular columns that define the circulation space within the inner curve of the U shape. The floor of the offices is raised to provide space for the cabling that is the ever-present companion of the IT office, and to form a plenum for the conditioned air that is introduced at floor level, Fig. 13.7.

BUILDING SERVICES

ENVIRONMENT

Like many other IT offices this building is fully air-conditioned. The noisy external environment and the depth of plan, made necessary by the con-straints of the site, made any other solution unreal-istic. There are four zones served from air handling units installed in the rooftop plant room. These zones are demarcated vertically, each one being a slice down through the three floors of offices; both the social amenities and the Computer Suite are separate individual zones. In addition to the air-conditioning system there are radiators installed around the perimeter to offset the heat loss and possible cold downdraughts; these have low tem-perature hot water circulating through them from a temperature compensated heating system and each one has a thermostatically controlled valve for individual adjustment.

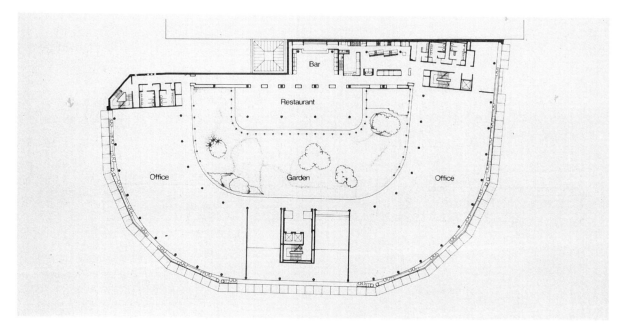

FIGURE 13.4 FIRST FLOOR PLAN

FIGURE 13.5 CIRCULATION CORRIDOR AND GLAZED WALL TO COURTYARD

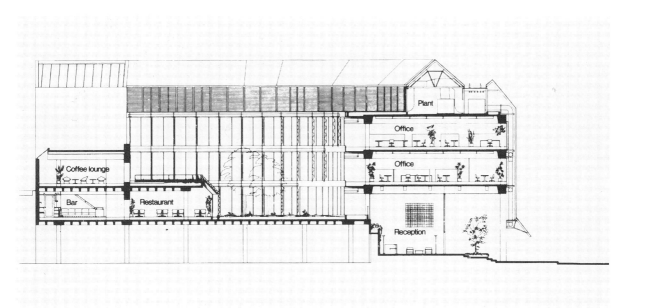

FIGURE 13.6 CROSS-SECTION

FIGURE 13.7 VIEW ACROSS OPEN PLAN OFFICES

CENTRAL PLANT ROOM

All the main components of the environmental control system are gathered together in a plant room at roof level. Gas fired boilers produce the low temperature hot water, and water chillers serve to cool water for the air-conditioning system; the cooling towers for the latter stand out on the roof itself. Lined out along the length of the plant room are the air handling units that provide the various zones with conditioned air.

Office Area 8500 m²

Boiler Output 700 kW

Chiller Capacity, approx 400 kW

SOLAR WALL

The glass curtain wall that has been referred to as a 'fly sheet' has several functions, in addition to its primary role of buffer space to reduce the penetration of outside noise and reduce solar heat gain. It is also an integral part of the environmental control system, acting at times, when heat is needed, as a solar wall to provide a boost to the temperature of incoming outside air, and through its anti-sun glazing can be seen the red vertical ducts that carry the conditioned air. Within Kahn's definition it is therefore a 'servant space' as well as buffer space, Fig. 13.8.

There are three layers to the solar wall: the outer anti-sun planar structural glazing system; the motorized aluminium venetian blinds that are automatically controlled by solar cells, and the concrete frame of the building shell. In the warmer days of summer, when solar gain is excessive, the wall acts as a series of filters or switches. First the outer glazing attenuates the direct penetration, but in so doing its surface temperature rises. Next the venetian blinds cut out the glare and deflect the sun's rays, and finally the exposed concrete mass of the frame of the building absorbs both the direct radiation and the convected heat. This potential accumulation of heat would eventually soak into the offices themselves were it not for the fact that the gap in the wall is ventilated by its stack effect, the resulting hot air rising up into the plant room and discharging out of louvred openings on the north side to be replaced with outside coming in from below through the canopy over the shop fronts.

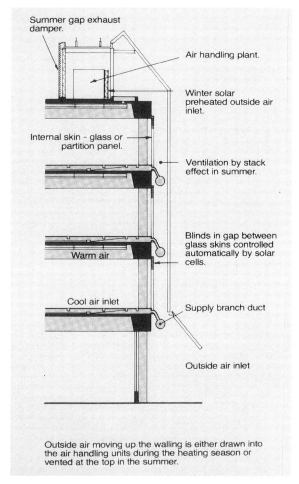

FIGURE 13.8 SOLAR WALL, CROSS-SECTION

Labels on figure:
Summer gap exhaust damper.
Air handling plant.
Winter solar preheated outside air inlet.
Internal skin - glass or partition panel.
Ventilation by stack effect in summer.
Blinds in gap between glass skins controlled automatically by solar cells.
Warm air
Cool air inlet
Supply branch duct
Outside air inlet

Outside air moving up the walling is either drawn into the air handling units during the heating season or vented at the top in the summer.

In the winter, outside air is drawn up through the cavity of the wall and into the plant room by the action of the fans in the air handling units. The air, now pre-warmed on its route up the wall by solar radiation and by the heat escaping through the fabric of the building, is then taken into the air handling units to reduce the heating load, Fig. 13.9.

AIR DISTRIBUTION

Conditioned air leaves the air handling unit and is ducted down through the gap between the outer glass and the building proper. Twin ducts drop side by side to serve their particular zone. As they reach each floor level a branch duct is taken off to meet with a boot connection that is attached to an entry point in the raised floor. Air is then introduced into

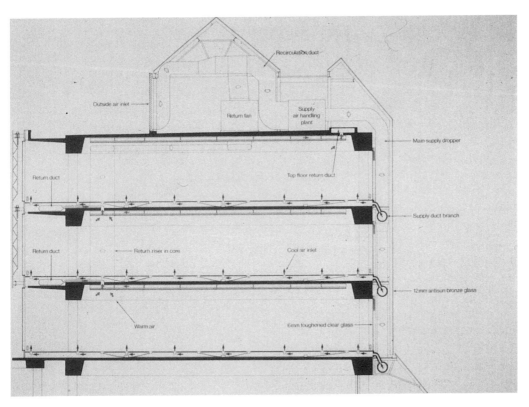

FIGURE 13.9 INTEGRATION OF BUILDING AND SERVICES

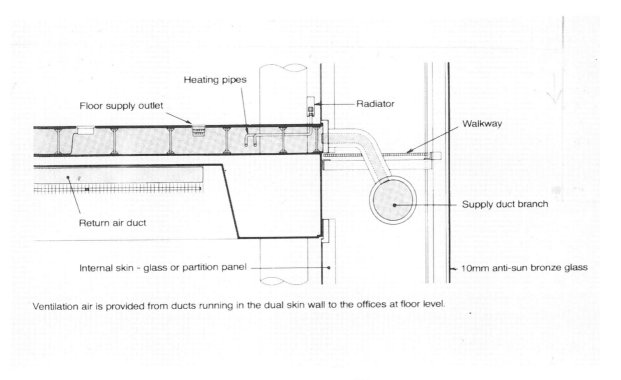

Ventilation air is provided from ducts running in the dual skin wall to the offices at floor level.

FIGURE 13.10 DETAIL OF RAISED FLOOR AND AIR DISTRIBUTION

the floor plenum, where it finds its way out into the offices in a Krantz twist type outlet, Fig. 8.3.

Supplying air at floor level has in the past not enjoyed great success, especially when cool air is being introduced. Either the air moves into the space too briskly, creating a useful pattern of air movement, but being experienced by the occupants as a draught, or it is introduced at a low speed so as not to cause thermal discomfort, but fails to stimulate sufficient movement of room air to offset complaints about 'stuffiness'.

These problems are largely overcome by the type of outlets used in Briarcliff House (and as you have seen, also in the offices for Royal Insurance). This unit creates a vortex in the air as it leaves it, and the action entrains room air, so although the leaving air speed is probably fairly high it rapidly reduces before coming in contact with any occupants. The action takes place entirely in the occupied zone, providing the necessary cooling where it is needed and because it is not designed to directly offset the heat emitted by the office machines and the lighting, less conditioned air is needed. After leaving the occupied zone the air drifts up to troughs between the beams and is drawn back over the light fittings into a return duct attached to the soffit of the slab. From there it travels in a duct above the ceiling of the circulation corridor to the service core and then rises back to the air handling unit for partial recirculation or discharge to outside.

The use of the raised floor as a plenum chamber, combined with the twist outlets, provides flexiblity in the arrangement of furniture. Outlets may be turned off or moved to another part of the floor and, because they are distributed over the whole of the office area, if some are covered by the importune placing of furniture there will be little deterioration in the overall performance, Fig. 13.10.

INTEGRATION

Arup Associates, like their originator, have adopted conceptual and functional integration over many years. According to one critic, it 'has become not only a tightly knit pattern of ducts and beams demarking circulation, but the fabric of the building and the air-conditioning have been brought together in symbiosis which offers a more stable environment' (Hanney, 1984). Unlike some of their other designs, this at Briarcliff House does not seek to stabilize the environment by using the potential flywheel action of the floor slab or by adopting the passive methodology of night-time cooling. However, it does use outer planar glass wall as a thermal stabilizer, and it does act in a symbiotic way as both buffer space and solar wall. Integration continues in the design of the wall as servant space and the floor as plenum. The whole has the unhurried logic of Arup Associates, combined with the feeling that nothing is wasted or done simply for effect.

CONCLUSION

Several people have written previously about this building, myself included, and it has inspired many student projects. Ironically the latter have always seen it as a passive solar building and adopted from it those components that have supported that view, but it was not designed as such. The solar wall is a by-product of the response to the problem of noise and solar gain, the latter being viewed initially as a nuisance rather than a benefit (this view can be seen to continue in the Case Study of the Royal Life Offices). Therefore the building carries an important message when designing passive solar buildings in the UK, for the solar wall did make a contribution to the cost of heating the building, but it made a similar contribution by also acting as a double-glazed unit and reducing heat loss. This bears out my own opinion that, where possible, a passive solar component should also offer some amenity value, solve a problem thrown up by the site or it should act in tandem with a design feature that is environmentally sensitive, e.g. an atrium, arcade or conservatory, or, as in this instance, a buffer space to reduce traffic noise.

CHAPTER FOURTEEN

CASE STUDY: ST MARY'S HOSPITAL

INTRODUCTION

The new St Mary's Hospital on the Isle of Wight is a design that was born out of a study commissioned in 1979 by the Department of Health. The department commissioned Building Design Partnership to lead a consortium of the Ahrends Burton & Koralek (ABK) architectural practice and structure engineers Gifford and Partners, to investigate the means of designing a low energy hospital. St Mary's is one of two prototype low-energy hospitals that the Department of Health decided to build as an outcome of those studies.

The aim of the study, and therefore the design strategy of the hospital, is fourfold:

- to reduce the demand for energy
- to explore means of recovering waste heat
- to investigate ways in which the outstanding demand for energy could be met efficiently
- to combine these concepts into an integrated energy strategy.

ABK were subsequently commissioned to design the hospital in 1981. The design is based on the Department of Health's planning method, known as the Nucleus template. It is on sloping ground, between the older hospital building and a small lake. Providing 200 beds, it covers a total of 17000m². In addition to the wards for the elderly and children, it includes four operating theatres, an accident and emergency department, pathology laboratories, pharmacy, offices, a kitchen and dining facilities. This case study is by necessity constrained and will highlight the way in which the wards were daylit as well as the provision of space for service. For a general description and discussion of the building see *Architects' Journal*, 3:7:91. (Davies, 1991)

DESCRIPTION

The Nucleus template has been devised by the Department of Health to expedite the design of hospital departments. The template is an all-purpose cruciform shape that may be divided up internally to suit various departmental functions; these are conventionally arranged to form an orthogonal grid. However, ABK departed from convention by arranging the templates on a curve. Fanned outward and climbing the contours of the site, they have as a common focal point the entrance and the central departments. The arms of the templates are linked by the inevitable hospital corridor, but – because of the break from the orthogonal – the usual endless vista is absent and there are occasional views out into innner courts. The radial plant effectively shortens the street and in that it is also the major services route it reduces the distance between the energy centre and the various departments. The building varies in section from two floors at the top of the site near the entrance to three floors at the lower part of the slope. Sandwiched between the floors is a service zone, which maintains a constant level from the energy centre and throughout all the templates. There is a second service level within the individual roofs of the templates.

BUILDING SERVICES

Environment

The wards of St Mary's (and several other areas) are designed to be free-running during the warmer months – without any air conditioning – and to be heated and mechanically ventilated in the winter. Some spaces obviously need more precise control and the maintenance of ultra clean conditions (the operating suite being a typical example), and these must be fully air conditioned. Others, such as the laboratories, need mechanical ventilation and a reliable extract system for items like fume cupboards. All of this was to be achieved against a background of designing to reduce the demand for energy below that set by an already efficient target.

Central Plant

Situated to the north of the site, and close to the focal point of the hub formed by the Nucleus templates, is the energy centre. It is some distance from the template on the southern wing, but nevertheless close to those parts of the hospital – the air conditioned operating suites, the pathology laboratory and the kitchen – that make the heaviest demands and are the most heavily serviced. Its position owes more to the strategy of exploring the means of recovering heat that would otherwise be wasted. The primary piped services are distributed from the energy centre within a main service zone. This is arranged to take advantage of the gradient of the site and runs at the same level as that of the energy centre throughout, therefore simplifying the path that the various pipes and cables take and thus reducing both capital and operating costs, Fig. 14.1. Following the path of the curved internal street, but entirely separate from the pedestrian traffic below, the route links the energy centre with the various departments. Heavily serviced zones, such as the operating suites, are served directly from this main service level – which occupies the full depth of the building and gives walking access for maintenance. This reduces to a minimum the need to gain access to services from the occupied and sometimes clinically sterile, spaces below, and lessens the risk of disruption that is the norm in many existing hospitals.

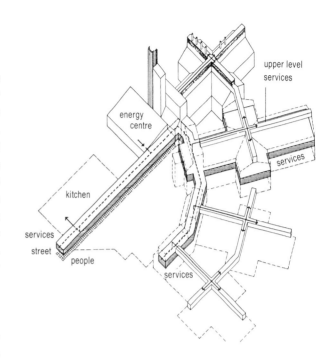

FIGURE 14.1 ENERGY CENTRE

The main service route connects the energy centre with the air-handling plant rooms that are located adjacent to the zones they serve. There are also local plant rooms at the roof level of the templates to serve the wards. The service routes for these areas are also designed to separate the services from the occupied spaces they serve, and to give walk-in access for ease of maintenance and the future installation of any additional equipment.

ENERGY CONSERVATION

Apart from being a working hospital, St Mary's is also a test bed of ideas about energy conservation. The initial study showed that lighting demanded most energy by taking 30 per cent of the primary energy, followed closely by that for fan and pump power. By contrast, the fabric losses only demanded 4 per cent of the total demand for primary energy. Therefore, although the u-value of the fabric is between 0.25 to 0.3 $W/m^2°C$, and attention was paid to reducing infiltration losses, the greatest savings in energy consumption are made by the best use of daylight and natural ventilation.

Another aim of the study was to recover waste heat. Waste heat in warm air may be discharged by the mechanical ventilation system. It is also dumped by the condenser sets of refrigeration systems, in the waste gases from high temperature incinerators and, to a less extent heat, by the water going down the drains. At St Mary's the energy that this wastage represents is reduced to a minimum by various recovery systems. Much of it is in the form of low-grade heat and it is recovered for use by heat pumps. These are driven by gas-fired electricity generators which also serve as the stand-by generators used in the case of a failure in mains supply. Strictly speaking, this is not true co-generation but it does give similar economic advantages. There is a saving in primary energy, while lower operating costs are obtained while making the otherwise wasted low-grade energy useful. And, furthermore, an economically favourable balance between the supply of gas and electricity was maintained by driving the generators with natural gas.

Peaks and troughs in the demand for heat, which could otherwise threaten the efficiency of the system, are smoothed out by using the recovered energy to heat water in medium- and high-temperature hot water storage tanks. In addition to upgrading recovered heat, the heat pumps also function as part of the orthodox vapour compression refrigeration cycle and serve the chiller needed for air conditioning. The temperature of the recovered heat from the waste products ranges from that coming off the flue of the incinerator at about 1000 degrees C, down to that of the water draining out of the kitchen (the recovery of which is done more for the sake of research than economy). Such a wide range cannot be handled efficiently by one single system – and therefore there are several, each matched to suit the condition of the source. Very hot air from the incinerator flue heat exchanger gives up its heat to the water in the high-temperature storage tank. Low temperature heat deriving from the waste water, the condenser sets of the refrigeration units and the vitiated air discharged to atmosphere is up-graded by the heat pumps and goes to the medium temperature tank. All of these energy conserving processes are controlled by the building energy management system.

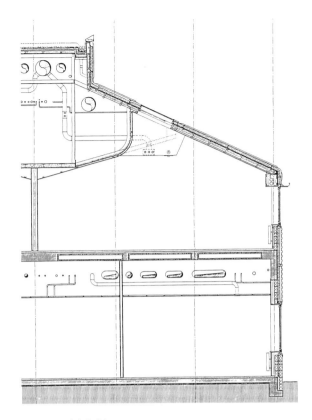

FIGURE 14.2 UPPER FLOORS

INTEGRATION

Louis Kahn's design for the Richards Memorial Laboratories made especial provision for the building services with his servant space towers, but when the pipes and ducts arrived inside things began to go wrong. This can not be allowed to happen in a hospital, where a failure or a simple mistake in the labelling of a piped service can be a life or death affair. Service routes are carefully planned and integrated into the whole of the building. They are not *ad hoc* afterthoughts, but sit within the structure as part of the whole and – in the case of the wards on the upper floor – their enclosure has a shape that works with the daylighting design and provides some visual variety. There is space to spare in the main service zones and this may be considered as an overindulgence, but medicine is at the cutting edge of science and the services system must be capable of change without causing disruption. The space is necessary so that the demands of change can be met.

LIGHTING

Overall the building is delightfully daylit, but it is inevitable with the Nucleus template that some parts, especially at the thicker nodes of the cruciform and the lower levels, are further away from the windows. The clinical wards on the upper floor have the benefit of top lighting, and it is these that are the most successful. Here the ceiling follows the slope of the pitched roof until it joins the curve of the bulkhead which conceals the service zone above; the curve is not unlike the bottom of a small boat viewed from below (which is properly appropriate for a hospital on the Isle of Wight). Light coming through rooflights to close to the join of roof and bulkhead is reflected off the curve and on to the ceiling (Fig. 14.2). The result is an excellent distribution of light and a feeling of spaciousness, out of proportion to the height of the room. To reduce the potential nuisance that may be caused by glare from the rooflights, electrically-operated blinds are fitted within them.

Mixed Mode Operation

The environmental control system for the wards is a typical mixed-mode arrangement. There are simple radiators mounted on the external walls. These are part of the reduced temperature, climate-sensitive controlled heating system and also have individual thermostatically controlled valves. In addition there is a mechanical ventilation system which provides an air change rate of 2/h and introduces air that, when heat is necessary, is preheated to between 10 to 16 degrees C. Air is extracted via the adjoining service rooms and passes through a heat-recovery section of the air handling unit, before being exhausted to outside.

During the summer the windows may be opened by either patients or the staff. Should the combination of openable windows and the tempting effect of the exposed internal mass of the building be insufficient to keep the temperature within acceptable limits in very hot weather, then the mechanical ventilation may be used to provide some additional cooling effect. In the winter, when the radiators are being used, the windows will be opened only rarely and the need for ventilation would be met entirely by the mechanical system.

CONCLUSION

Integration, both conceptual and functional, is at the heart of St Mary's. It is present in the way the template has been placed on the site to open up courtyards to the sun and provide a change to the hospital corridor, in the provision for services and how this comes together with the design for daylighting. The separation of served and servant spaces is essential in a hospital, to facilitate maintenance and safeguard the necessary standards of hygiene. At St Mary's it has been achieved with style. Critics have likened the building – with its stainless steel profile sheet cladding – to a machine, but it is doubtlessly a machine to help the sick to live.

CHAPTER FIFTEEN

CASE STUDY:
THE ANVIL CONCERT HALL

INTRODUCTION

The Renton Howard Wood Levin Partnership (RHWL) have a track record of designing auditoria that are capable of responding to the different needs of the performing arts, providing a friendly focus for the community and a valuable facility for commerce. This latest project, the Anvil Concert Hall, promises to live up to the practice's past achievements.

Sited in Basingstoke, Hampshire, the building is first and foremost a concert hall to seat some 1400 people, but it is designed to be capable of providing a venue for a wide range of functions. Its immediate neighbour is a shopping mall. Set among the day-to-day life of the community, it is a sure sign that this is meant to be arts for the people and not simply for the cognoscenti.

DESCRIPTION

Entrance into the building may be gained directly from Basingstoke's central shopping mall and car park or, more interestingly, across a footbridge that was purpose-designed for the project and spans over the road from nearby Church Street. The drum shape of a box office stands to one side of the entrance and to the other side is a bar with its traditional 'crush' plus a small outside terrace and small kitchen. Ahead is the foyer, a small multi-purpose hall, the usual cloaks and public toilets. The audience will enter on either side of the auditorium at the rear and facing the stage, going

directly into the stalls or up one flight to the balcony, the seating of which runs all around the perimeter, including a number of seats that are backstage that will be used on occasion for choral performances and the like, Fig. 15.1.

There are the familiar ancillary spaces: dressing rooms, rooms for the orchestra, individual rooms for the conductor and the soloists, offices, store rooms, and even one called intriguingly 'Reduced Chorus'. Most of these will double as seminar rooms when the building is being used for a conference. At the upper level is the Technical Gallery, with its Dimmer Room and catwalks giving access to the stage lighting and for maintenance.

As indicated earlier, although this is principally a concert hall it is, in a similar way to Northampton's Derngate Centre – also designed by RHWL – a multi-form space designed to adapt to various functions. It can provide a traditional proscenium arch that unfolds out of the floor of the stage for opera or ballet, a thrust stage or platform for conferences, or no stage at all and a flat floor for banquets.

Standing at what looks like the prow of this building is the Service Tower, separated from and effectively detached from the building it serves. Housed within it on five different levels, one on top of the other, are the air handling units, and topping it all off on the roof of the tower is the chiller of the air-conditioning system. Not designed as such, it is nevertheless an unconscious tribute to the Kahn philosophy of servant and served spaces.

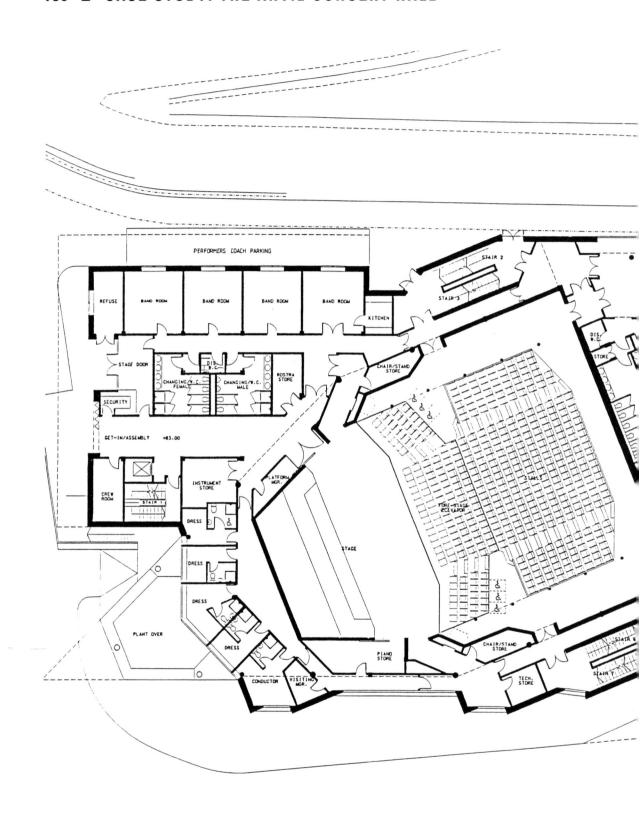

FIGURE 15.1 PLAN, ENTRANCE/STALLS LEVEL

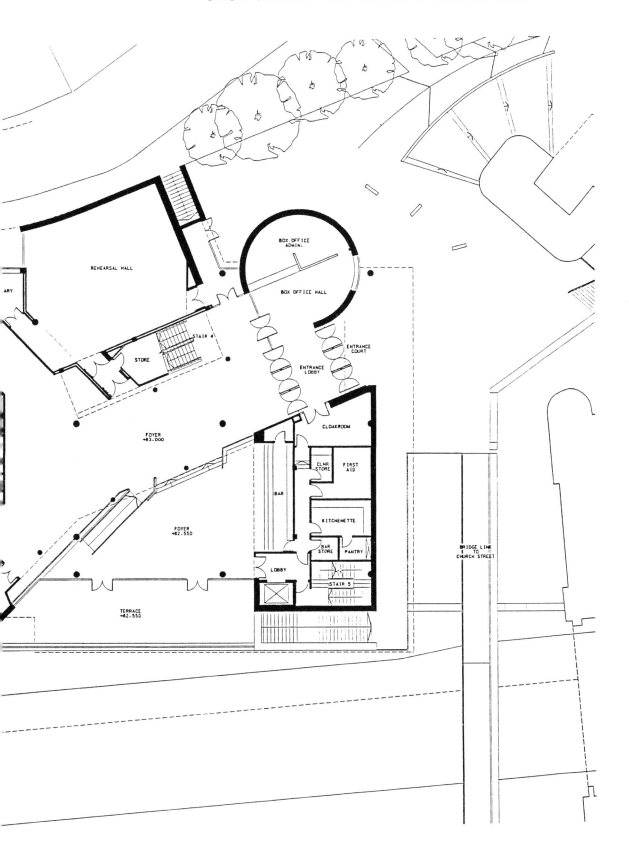

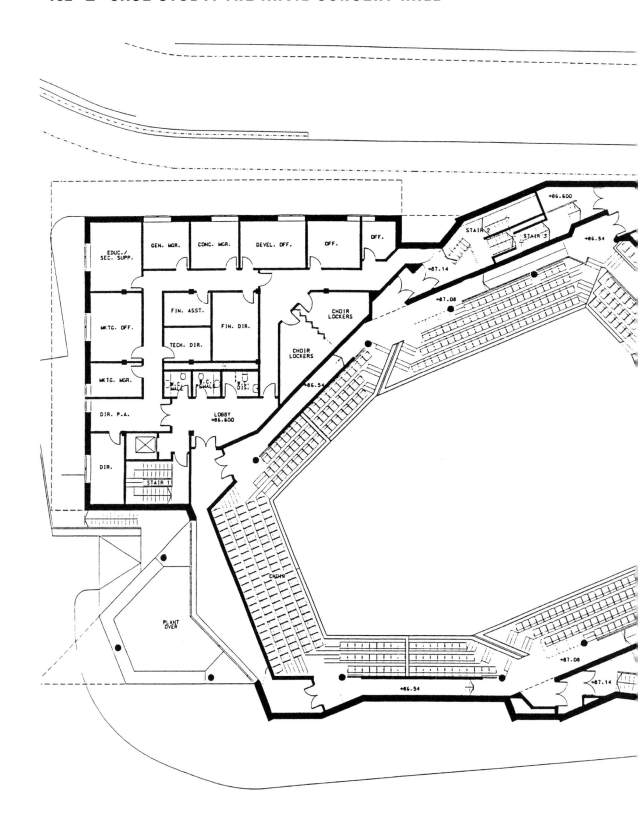

FIGURE 15.2 PLAN, UPPER FOYER/BALCONY

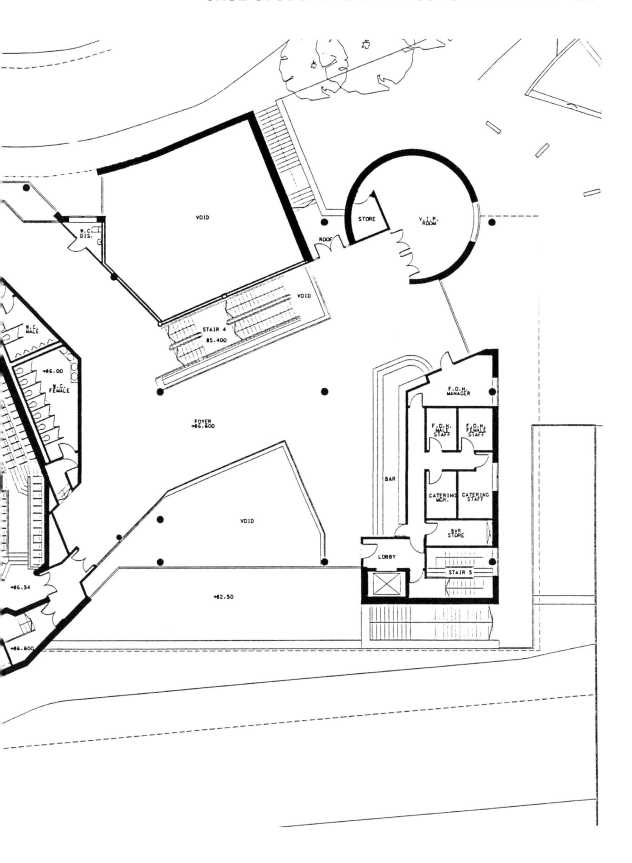

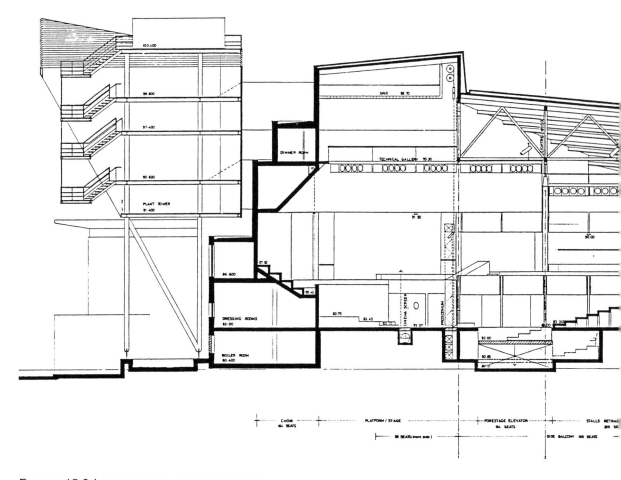

FIGURE 15.3 LONGITUDINAL CROSS-SECTION

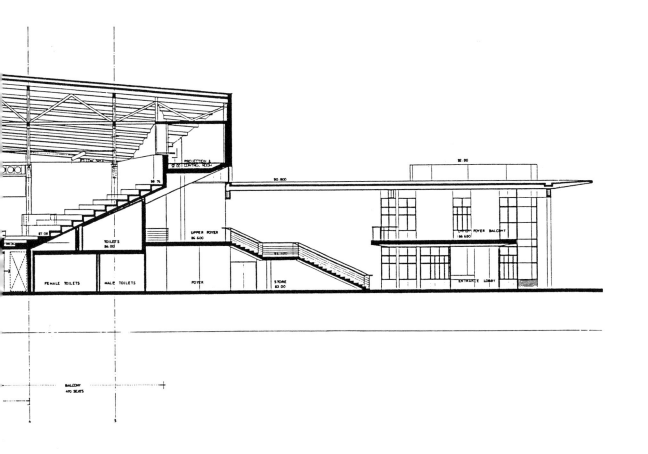

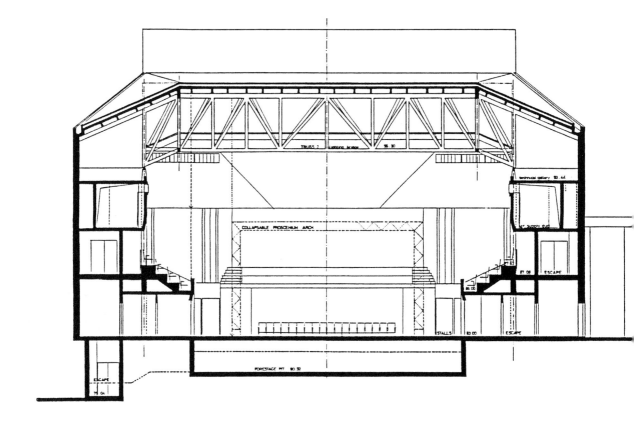

SECTION   D-D

FIGURE 15.4 CROSS-SECTIONS, D–D VIEW TO STAGE: E–E VIEW TO AUDIENCE

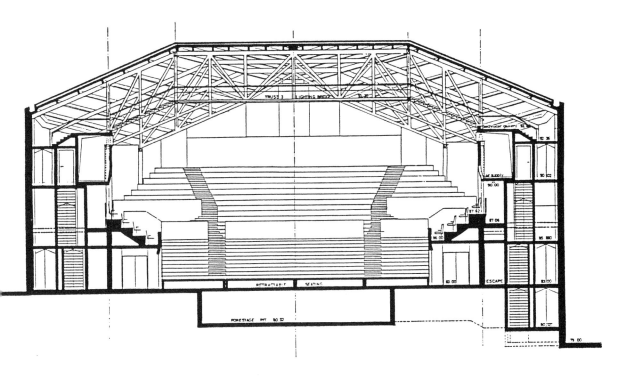

SECTION   E-E

CONCERT

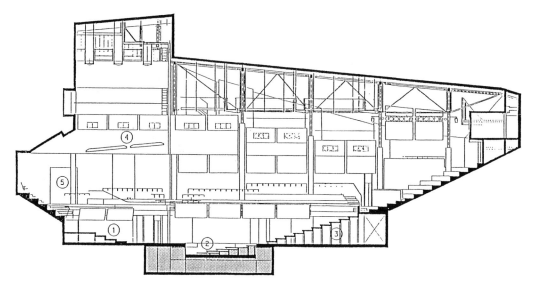

1 Orchestra riser in use
2 Elevator at seating level
3 Retractable seating in use
4 Orchestra reflectors in use
5 Choir

FIGURES 15.5–8 ARRANGEMENTS OF THE MULTI-FORM SPACE

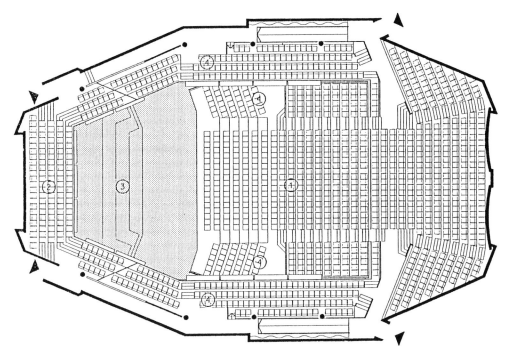

1 1226/1164 seats [1376 seats total]
2 150/212 choir
3 100 orchestra
4 12 disabled

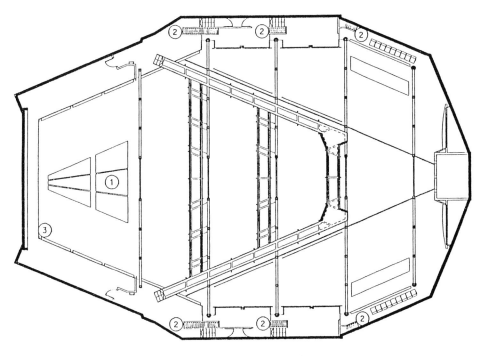

1 Orchestra reflectors and lighting in use
2 All acoustic curtains re-tracted
3 No stage drapes

PROSCENIUM
WITH ORCHESTRA PIT

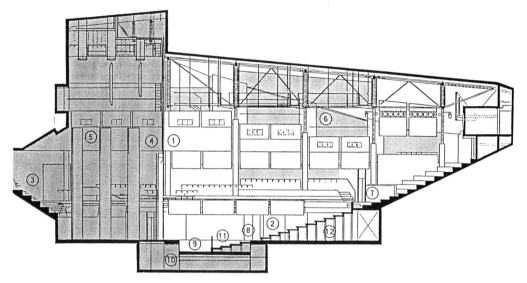

1 Proscenium arch and wall in use
2 928 seats
3 Choir not in use
4 House curtain
5 Stage masking
6 Acoustic curtains in use
7 Optional sound mixing position
8 6 Disabled
9 Orchestra pit
10 Orchestral riser in store
11 Elevator at seating level
12 Retractable seating in use

FIGURE 15.6

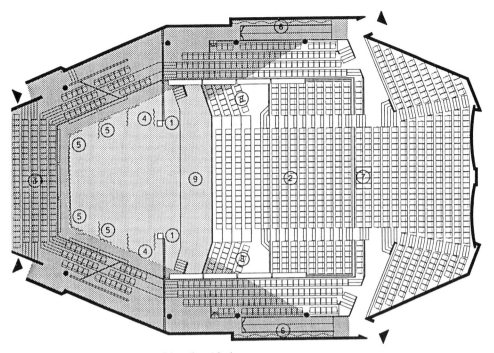

1 Proscenium arch and wall in position
2 928 seats
3 Choir not in use
4 House curtain
5 Stage masking

6 Acoustic curtains in use
7 Optional sound mixing position
8 6 Disabled
9 Orchestra pit

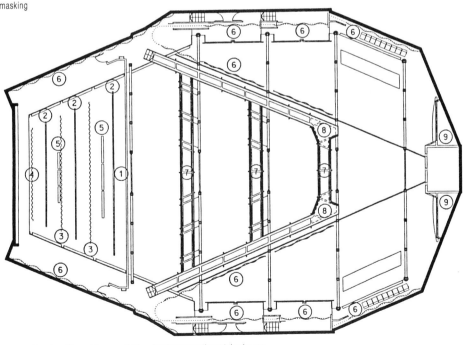

1 Proscenium arch and wall in position
2 3 lighting bars in use
3 2 borders in use
4 Backcloth in use
5 Orchestral reflectors stored

6 All auditorium acoustic curtains in use
7 Lighting bridge in use
8 Follow spot position in use
9 Control rooms in use

ARENA

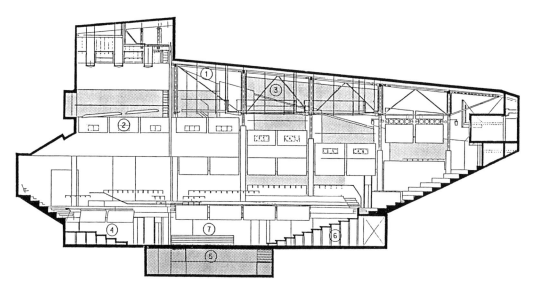

1 Additional suspension points
2 Orchestra reflectors at high level
3 50–100% of acoustic curtains in use
4 Orchestra riser raised
5 Elevator raised to flat floor
6 Retractable seating in use
7 Elevator rostra rotated through 90°

FIGURE 15.7

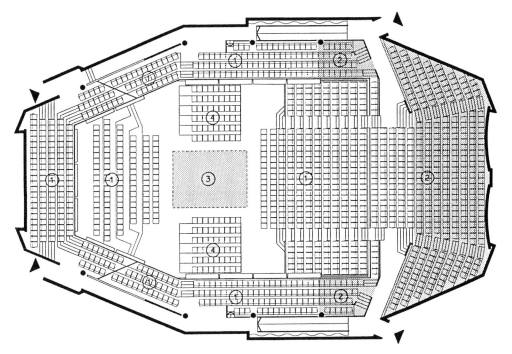

1 1020 seats
2 1392 seats full capacity
3 Flat floor performance area
4 Elevator rostra rotated through 90°

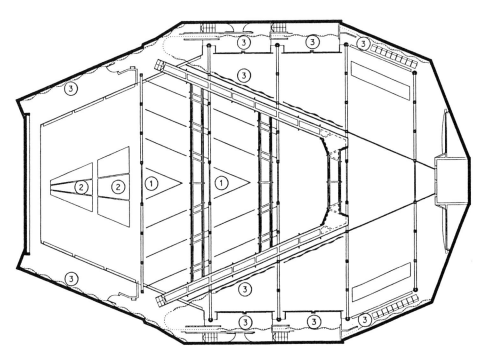

1 Additional suspension points
2 Orchestra reflectors at high level
3 50%–100% of acoustic curtains in use

FLAT FLOOR
BANQUETING AND EXHIBITION

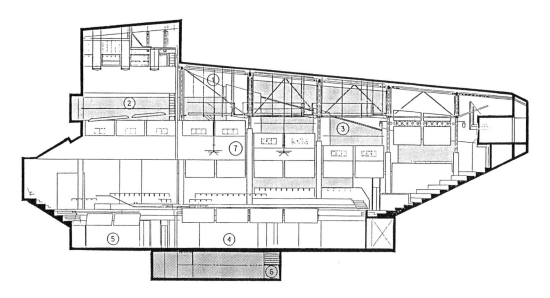

1 Additional suspension points
2 Orchestra reflectors at high level
3 Acoustic curtains in use
4 Elevator raised to flat floor
5 Orchestra risers in store
6 Retractable seating in store
7 Banqueting chandeliers

FIGURE 15.8

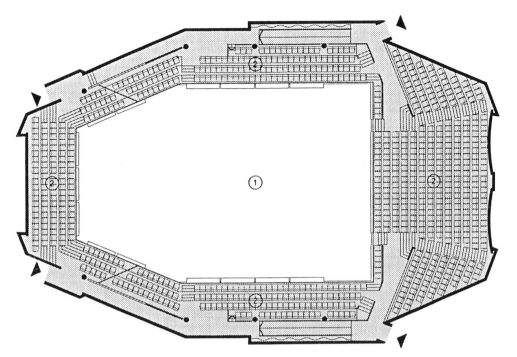

1 Flat floor banqueting/exhibition area 520m²
2 Upper level seating not in use

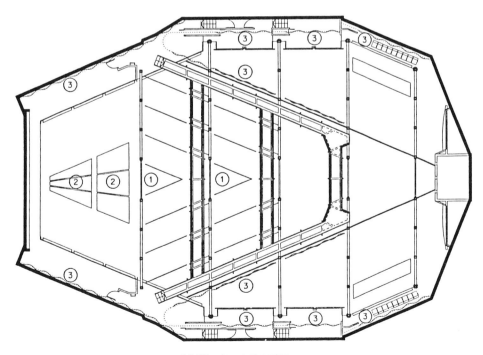

1 Additional suspension points
2 Orchestra reflectors at high level
3 Acoustic curtains in use

ACOUSTICS

Arup Associates, in the words of Richard Cowell, aimed to create 'a building where the public will be able to enjoy the finest music in a hall with world class acoustics that will provide the scope to make high quality CD recordings'. To this end, working with the architects they developed the internal form of the hall starting from a possible set of simple shapes. These were first tested by building scale models and later, developing from those results, by 3-D computer models. The physical models were tested acoustically by introducing a spark source inside them and picking up the resulting sound in miniature microphones built into the seating positions. Small lasers were also used to investigate patterns of sound reflection, adding mirror card to replicate acoustic reflectors that would improve the quality and bounce the sound to all parts of the audience.

The results of the testing are to be seen in the clean line of the geometric shape of the auditorium. But the aim for high standards of acoustics goes further than determining the shape of the most dominant volume; it has affected constructional details and resulted in such things as the irregular spacing of the exposed concrete ribs of the roof. More noticeably it is also responsible for the semi-detached position of the ventilation plant room in the tower.

The acoustic 'shape' of the auditorium can be adjusted to suit the various functions of this multi-form building. When it is used as a concert hall an acoustic reflector is lowered to a position above the orchestra on stage, while banners which drape the side walls on other occasions are stored away completely in boxes at high level to secure a reverberation time of 1.9 to 2.1 seconds. For popular music a reverberation time between 1.55 to 1.75 seconds is needed, and the banners are unfurled and the reflectors are hoisted up to high level.

Even the ducts carrying the conditioned air which run at high level along both sides of the auditorium play their part in the development of the acoustic conditions. The supply duct, which lies lower than the extract duct, helps to reflect sound back down to the audience and the orchestra, and the air diffusers are arranged so that air is brought down and guided in its path over the orchestra when the acoustic reflectors are in their lower position: a perfect example of acoustics, the building and the ventilation system all working together, Figs 15.2–15.8.

BUILDING SERVICES

ENVIRONMENT

The demanding noise criteria of NR 20 has meant that great care has had to be taken with the design of the environmental control systems, and in the choice of the place for their accommodation, to ensure that any noise generated by the equipment does not reach the auditorium.

The auditorium is divided into three air-conditioned environmental control zones, these being chosen to suit the many functions the building has to fulfil. The condition of the air supplied to each zone may be adjusted to the density of occupation within it automatically in pre-programmed steps.

The other single large space for a seated audience, the Small Hall, is air-conditioned by a DX system, having its own air handling unit quite separate from that of the auditorium system. Elsewhere, with the exception of toilets and some landlocked stores, the occupied rooms are capable of being naturally ventilated.

BOILER PLANT

As part of the defensive acoustic strategy the boilers are tucked down in the basement, as far away as possible from the noise-sensitive auditorium. Within the boiler room there are four gas fired boilers, together with the circulating pumps for the low temperature hot water heating system, a calorifier served by the boilers to generate and store domestic hot water, water softening plant and the cold water storage tank which feeds a pumped water system. There are two boiler flues; these, being clad in polished stainless steel, leave the building and rise up outside to above roof level, accompanied for some of the way by a 'dummy flue'. The latter is simply a means of hiding and protecting service connections that feed into the plant room in the service tower, Fig. 15.9.

Adjacent to the boiler room are the switch room, space for the batteries for the emergency lighting, an electrical sub-station, gas meter room, lift shaft and motor room.

Space allocation: Boiler Room, total area = 60 m² inc. cold and hot water storage.

Space for boilers & pumps = 48 m² approx.

Boiler output: 4 in total, 2 of which are each rated at 226 kW and 2 at 274 kW.

Note: there are two flues, each minimum 400 mm internal diameter.

Cold Water Storage (pumped system) = 7600 litres, tank size 2 × 2 × 2 m.

Domestic Hot Water Calorifiers, 2 in total, capacity of each = 550 litres at 60°C, plus multi-point units.

CHILLER UNITS

Air cooled chiller (to auditorium) on Plant Tower
Roof   = 507 kW

Condensing unit (Small Hall) 1, rated output
     = 9.5 kW

Also, fan-coil unit to Box Office   Cooling 5 kW
     Heating 5.5 kW

DX unit to Amp Room   Cooling 4.8 kW
     Heating 6.2 kW

DX unit to Dimmer Room   Cooling 6.6 kW
     Heating 10.6 kW

Only the main auditorium is fully air-conditioned, and the water chiller unit that serves the cooling coils in the air handling unit sits high up on the top of the towers. Sited directly over the air handling unit, the circulation pipes from the chiller are kept as short as possible and pumping costs are low.

AIR HANDLING UNITS

The auditorium is air-conditioned by two air handling units installed within the service tower. These draw in outside air through a common grille inlet set in the face of the tower, on through an attenuator to mix it with recirculated air within the unit. At a level above the supply units are two further air handling units which either direct recirculated air to the supply units, or exhaust the vitiated air through yet another attenuator and out over the rooftop.

Each of the supply air units has within it three separate heating and cooling coils to provide controlled conditions for the zones within the auditorium. In addition there are several smaller air handling units serving various rooms, the largest of which serves the Small Hall and is situated in the smallest plant room possible – below a flight of stairs.

●   In addition there is the supply of air to the boiler room, a fan rated at 3.3 m³/s.

There are also several extract fans for the toilets, battery room, lift motor room, kitchen and the boiler room (see table below).

The noise criteria for the whole building is so demanding that every fan is fitted with a noise attenuator in its inlet and outlet. There are more than 50 attenuators, ranging from the largest in the supply and extract ducts of the auditorium system to the smallest with an air flow of 0.85 m³/s in the lift motor room extract fan.

Room Ventilated	AHU Output (m³/s)
Auditorium: supply	2 each at 8.4
	(Zone 1: 1.85. Zone 2: 4.65. Zone 3: 1.9)
extract	2 each at 8.4
Small Hall: supply/extract	1 at 1.5
Kitchen: supply only	1 at 0.9
Admin, Front House: supply only	1 at 0.2
Front House, toilets (with run-around coil) supply	1 at 0.85
extract	1 at 1.05
Control Room: supply/extract	1 at 0.38
Back House, ancillary: supply only	1 at 0.44

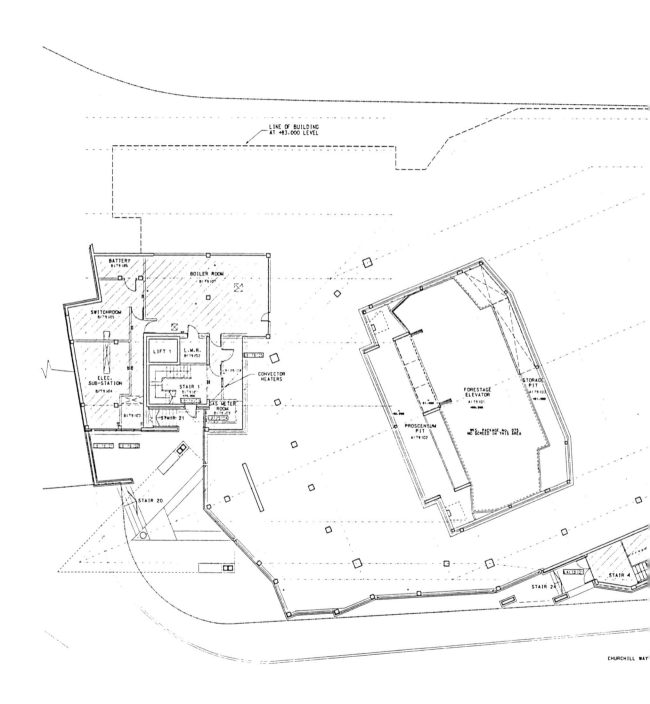

FIGURE 15.9 PLAN, BASEMENT AND BOILER ROOM

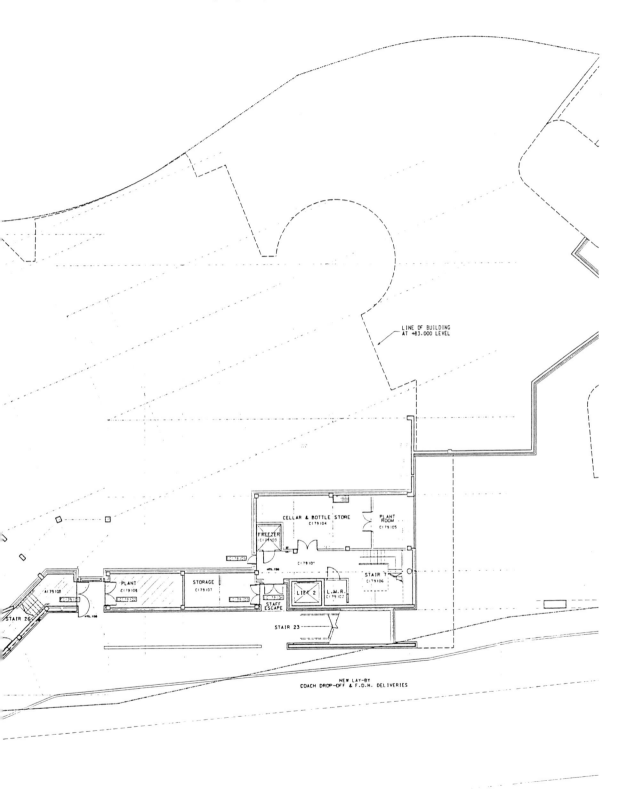

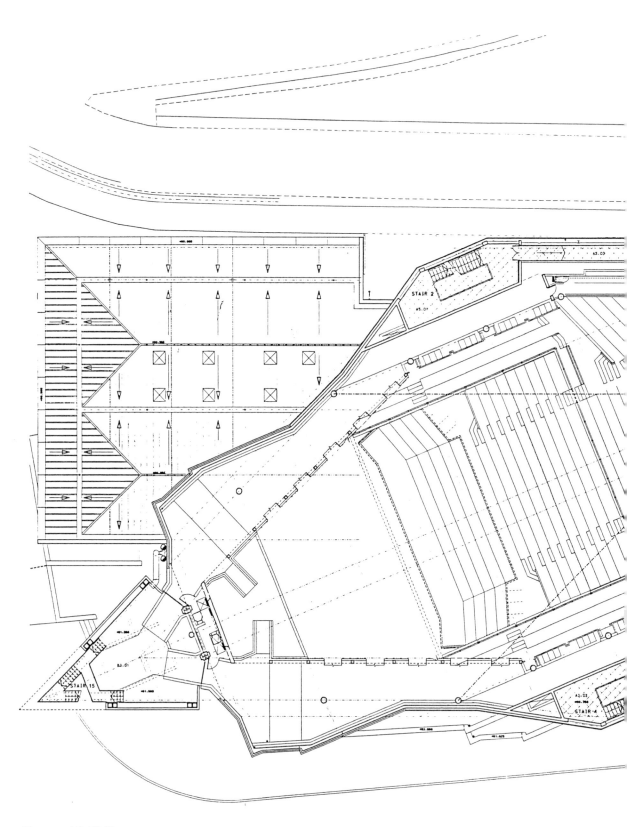

FIGURE 15.10 PLANT TOWER AND AIR SUPPLY DUCTS

AIR DISTRIBUTION

The NR specification of 20 has called for special care in the design and specification of the ventilation system. As has been mentioned earlier, the plant room for the air handling units is more or less separated from the building in a tower, where the units are mounted one above the other.

There are two supply air handling units, sitting side by side on the same level in the tower, each designed to condition and introduce air from opposite sides of the auditorium. The ducts from each of the units leave the tower diagonally to run at high level down opposite sites of the inside wall of the auditorium. Before leaving the plant room the supply air goes through the first of a series of attenuators and, on entering the building, passes through a second large attenuator, so large in fact that it would be possible to drive a Renault 5 through the opening that houses it.

The main supply ducts form part of the building structure and are sub-divided internally to provide separate conduits for each of the three zones. To ensure that the air flow does not generate noise in its passage through the ducts its velocity is much lower than is the case in other types of buildings and is about 1–2 metres per second.

Conditioned air in the duct leaves by way of acoustically treated air scoops that direct the air into supply diffusers. The diffusers are arranged in banks in the sides of the main duct, pushing the air down into the auditorium, well above the audience but below any possible bouyant effect of the stage lighting.

Air is extracted in a much more direct fashion, being taken out of the space at high level through grilles at the stage end of the auditorium and directed through ducts set above the supply ducts into the plant tower, Fig. 15.10.

CONCLUSION

With one possible exception, Basingstoke is a place of downright ugly office buildings. Betjeman might have even coupled it with Slough when he called for those 'friendly bombs' to fall. Perhaps the Anvil Theatre will begin to put matters right.

The success of the design of this building is largely due to an integrated effort. Starting with the close co-operation of the architect and the acoustic consultant, who together created the shape of the building, it continued into an understanding partnership with the structural and the building services engineers. The evidence of the integrated design is shown principally in the auditorium, where the components of its construction and environmental built form work so well together, and their individual contribution extends beyond convention.

The Anvil Concert Hall was chosen as the final Case Study because it is an example where so much of what this book is about has been put to use. The architecture fulfils the function and yet loses nothing by doing so. There is properly allocated space for the services, and that space is celebrated rather than put aside. The building services engineer understood the problem and designed a well thought out system that is elegant in its simplicity and yet totally at one with the acoustical demands of a top class concert hall.

APPENDIX

THE CHECK LIST

This is intended as an *aide-mémoire* as you progress through a design project. Although it is shown as a sequential process this is simply because it is easier to write it in that manner; you will no doubt find yourself referring to it in a completely different way to suit your own design method. The list should help you find the information that you need faster than ploughing through the book chapter by chapter.

ASSESSMENT AIDS

These reflect my own personal interest in such things, but if you need a starting point for an assessment of whether the building that you are designing needs air-conditioning or not, they should be useful. You may doubt the value that I have given to certain features, but they are based on my own longish experience, together with information from reliable sources, and I recommend them as an early design aid.

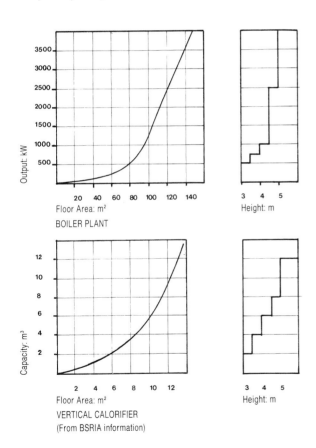

BOILER PLANT

VERTICAL CALORIFIER
(From BSRIA information)

SPACE ALLOCATION FOR BOILER PLANT

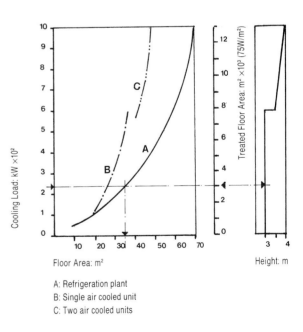

A: Refrigeration plant
B: Single air cooled unit
C: Two air cooled units

SPACE ALLOCATION FOR REFRIGERATION EQUIPMENT

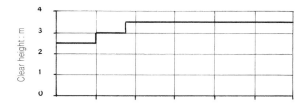

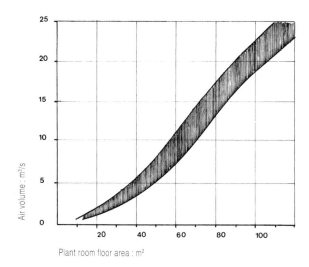

SPACE ALLOCATION FOR AIR HANDLING UNIT

CHECK LIST

DESIGN PROCESS	RESOURCE
Analysis of use Identify activities and any internal constraints	Brief/Design program
Appraisal of Site Climate, topology, solar access. Identify external constraints, access to site, adjacent buildings.	Chapter Two
Generate and Test Built Form Options	Chapter One
Identify Use and Need Zones	Chapter Three Performance Specification Fig. 3.3
Assess.Built Form for Ventilation and Daylight Test against built form options	Chapter Two Assessment Aids 1 and 2 Nomogram Fig. 2.7.
Evaluate Design of Fenestration for Daylight and Solar Access Consider solar control options	Chapter Two Assessment Aid 1
Formulate Environmental Control Strategy Evaluate against Needs and Use, client's	Chapter Four Fig. 4.1 Assessment Aid 2
Consider Constructional Mass Compare with the needs of any passive solar strategy	Chapter Two
Match Possible Environmental Control Systems to Needs and Use Zones	
Heating only	Chapter Five
Heating and mechanical ventilation	Chapter Six
Comfort cooling	Chapter Seven
Air-conditioning	Chapter Seven
Allocate Space for Systems	
Boilers	Fig. 4.6
Air handling units	Fig. 4.16
Refrigeration	Fig. 4.11
Cooling towers	Fig. 4.11
Hot water calorifiers	Fig. 4.6
Service cores	Fig. 4.19

ASSESSMENT AIDS

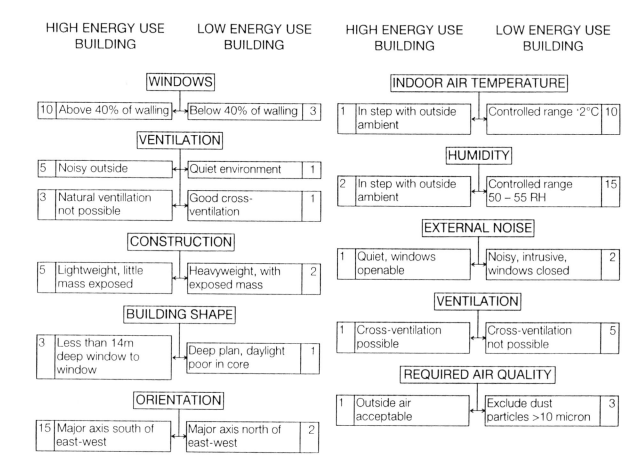

HIGH ENERGY USE BUILDING	LOW ENERGY USE BUILDING
WINDOWS	
10 Above 40% of walling	Below 40% of walling 3
VENTILATION	
5 Noisy outside	Quiet environment 1
3 Natural ventillation not possible	Good cross-ventilation 1
CONSTRUCTION	
5 Lightweight, little mass exposed	Heavyweight, with exposed mass 2
BUILDING SHAPE	
3 Less than 14m deep window to window	Deep plan, daylight poor in core 1
ORIENTATION	
15 Major axis south of east-west	Major axis north of east-west 2

HIGH ENERGY USE BUILDING	LOW ENERGY USE BUILDING
INDOOR AIR TEMPERATURE	
1 In step with outside ambient	Controlled range ·2°C 10
HUMIDITY	
2 In step with outside ambient	Controlled range 50 – 55 RH 15
EXTERNAL NOISE	
1 Quiet, windows openable	Noisy, intrusive, windows closed 2
VENTILATION	
1 Cross-ventilation possible	Cross-ventilation not possible 5
REQUIRED AIR QUALITY	
1 Outside air acceptable	Exclude dust particles >10 micron 3

This diagram may be used at the strategic stage of design to assess the built form and the possible need for environmental control systems. The rankings given are arbitary and may be modified to suit local conditions and the function of the building.

Add the values given to aid assessment as shown below:

Total:
1–19: Good natural environment
20–29: Summer weather may cause problems, consider solar control
30–39: Air conditioning will be necessary
Above 40: Make modifications to design

Derived from BRE data

This diagram may be used at the strategic design stage to assess the need for mechanical ventilation and/or air conditioning. The rankings given are only arbitary and may be modified to suit local conditions and the function of the building.

Add the values given to aid assessment as shown below:

Total:
1–6: Natural ventilation and simpler heating system acceptable
8–16: Mechanical ventilation needed, indoor temperatures may be above comfort level
17–25: Partial control needed of temperature and RH at peak, comfort cooling possible
26: Full air conditioning necessary

FURTHER READING & REFERENCES

AJ, 'Focus Case Study: Foster's Frames', *Architects' Journal*, May 1989, pp. 19–22

Alexander, Christopher, *Notes on the Synthesis of Form*, Harvard University Press, Cambridge, Massachusetts, 1971

Archer, Bruce, 'Systematic Methods for Designers', *Design*, 172, 174, 176, 179, 181, 185, 188, April–August 1963–4

Arup Associates, *Arup Journal*, Autumn 1991, pp. 3–10

Banham, Reyner, *The Architecture of the Well-Tempered Environment*, Architectural Press, London, 1969

Bedford, T., 'Environmental Warmth and its Measurement', War Memorandum No. 17, Medical Research Council, HMSO 1940/1961

Brown, G.Z., *Sun, Wind and Light*, John Wiley, New York, 1985

BSRIA, *Technical Appraisal 1/90*, Part 2: 'Selection Procedure', Building Services Research and Information Association, Bracknell, 1990

BSRIA, *Technical Note 8*, Building Services and Information Association, Bracknell, 1992a

BSRIA, *Technical Note TN10/92*, Building Services Research and Information Association, Bracknell, 1992b

Burberry, P. and Eastop, T.D., *Environmental Services*, 7th edn, Longman, London, 1992

Burke, James, *Connections*, Macmillan, London, 1978

Chadderton, D., and Lord, P. *Air Conditioning*, E & F N Spon, London, 1993

Chandler, T.J., *The Climate of London*, Hutchinson, London, 1965

CIBSE, *Applications Manual AM3*, Chartered Institute of Building Services Engineers, London, 1989

CIBSE, *CIBSE Guide*, Chartered Institute of Building Services Engineers, London, 1970

Commission of the European Communities, 'Briarcliff House', in: *Project Monitor*, No. 12, December 1987

Cuff, Dana, *Architecture, the Story of Practice*, MIT Press, Cambridge, Massachusetts, 1991

De Bono, Edward, *Lateral Thinking for Management*, Penguin Books, London, 1971

Department of Energy, *Good Practice Guide 16*, 1990

Evans, Barrie, 'Summer Cooling – Using Thermal Capacity', *Architects' Journal*, 12 August 1992, pp. 38–41

Evans, Martin, *Housing, Climate and Comfort*, Architectural Press, London, 1980

Forrester, John, 'Designing: Making Sense Together in Practical Conversations', *Journal of Architectural Education*, Vol. 38, No. 3, 1985, pp. 14–20.

Gidlow, Peter, 'Blowing Hot and Cold', *Heating and Air Conditioning*, July 1991

Givoni, B., *Man, Climate and Architecture*, Applied Science, London, 1981

Goulding, John R. (ed.), *Energy Conscious Design – A Primer for Architects*, Batsford, London, 1992

Goulding, John R., Lewis, J. Owen & Steemers, Theo C., *Energy in Architecture: The European Passive Solar Handbook*, Batsford, London, 1993

Griffiths, J., *Thermal Comfort in Buildings with Passive Solar Features, Final Report to CEC*, University of Surrey, 1990.

Guedes, P. (ed.), *The Macmillan Encyclopaedia of Architecture and Technological Change*, Macmillan, London, 1979, p. 205

Hanney, Patrick, 'Farnborough Salute', *Architects' Journal*, 5 September 1984, pp. 63–9

Harrison, J. et al, 'Sick Building Syndrome – Further prevalence studies', Conference Proceedings: *Indoor Air*, 1987

Hawkes, D., 'Building Shape and Energy', in: Hawkes, D. & Owers, J., *The Architecture of Energy*, Construction Press, Harlow, 1982, pp. 22–34

Heath, Tom, *Method in Architecture*, John Wiley, New York, 1984

Hopkinson, R.G. & Kay, J.D., *The Lighting of Buildings*, Heinemann, London, 1966

Houghten, F.C. & Yaglou, C.P., 'Determination of the Comfort Zone', *Trans. ASHVE*, Vol. 29, 1923, p. 361

Humphreys, M.A., *Field Studies of Thermal Comfort Compared and Applied*, BRE Current Paper 76/75, 1975

Jones, John Chris, *Design Methods*, 2nd edn, Van Nostrand Reinhold, New York, 1966

Knevitt, Charles, *The Responsive Office, People and Change*, Polymath, Streatley-on-Thames, 1990

Koenigsberger, O.H. et al, *Manual of Tropical Housing and Building*, Part 1, Longman, London, 1973

Lam, William M.C., *Sunlighting as a Form-giver for Architecture*, Van Nostrand Reinhold, New York, 1986

Laseau, Paul, *Graphical Thinking for Architects and Designers*, Van Nostrand Reinhold, New York, 1980

Littlefair, P.J., *Site Layout Planning for Daylight and Sunlight*, BRE Report, 1991

Lloyd Wright, Frank, *The Natural House*, Horizon Press, New York, 1954

Love, J., 'Naturally Greener', *Building Services and Environmental Engineer*, December 1992

Lovelock, James, *Gaia. The Practical Science of Planetary Medicine*, QPD, London, 1991

Markus, T.A. & Morris, E.N., *Buildings, Climate and Energy*, Pitman, London, 1980

Martin, P.L. and Oughton, D.R., *Faber & Kell's Heating and Air Conditioning of Buildings*, 7th edn, Butterworth, London, 1989

Mazria, Edward, *The Passive Solar Energy Book*, Rodale Press, Emmaus, 1979

McGinty, Tim, 'Concepts in Architecture', in: Snyder, J.C. & Catanese, A.J. (eds), *Introduction to Architecture*, McGraw-Hill, New York, 1979, pp. 208–37

McMullan, R., *Environmental Science in Buildings*, Macmillan, London, 1992

Moore, Fuller, *Concepts and Practice of Architectural Lighting*, Van Nostrand Reinhold, New York, 1985

Myers, N. (ed.), *Gaia: An Atlas of Planet Management*, Doubleday, New York, 1984

Nelson, G. & Stamp, G., 'A Modern Classic', *Architects' Journal*, 26 September 1984

Nelson, Gordon, 'The Glass of '84', *Architects' Journal*, 5 September 1984, pp. 70–82

Neufort, F., *Neufort Architects' Data*, Blackwells Scientific Publications, Oxford, 1980

Norberg-Schulz, C, *Intentions in Architecture*, MIT Press, Cambridge, Massachusetts, 1968

Olgyay, V., *Design with Climate*, Princetown University Press, 1963

Olley, John & Wilson, Caroline, 'The Natural History Museum', in: Cruickshank, Dan (ed.) *Timeless Architecture*, Vol. 1, Architectural press, London, 1985

Orton, Andrew, *The Way We Build Now: Form, Scale and Technique*, E & F N Spon, London, 1988

Penwarden A.D., *Wind Environment Around Buildings*, Building Research Establishment, 1975

Reid, D., *Understanding Buildings*, Longman, London, 1984

Rowe, Peter G., *Design Thinking*, MIT Press, Cambridge, Massachusetts, 1991

Rush, Richard (ed.), *The Building Systems Integration Handbook*, John Wiley, New York, 1986

Saxon, Richard, *Atrium Buildings – Development and Design*, Architectural Press, London, 1983

Stein, R.G., *Architecture and Energy*, Anchor press, New York, 1977

Stevens, Garry, *The Reasoning Architect: Mathematics and Science in Design*, McGraw-Hill, New York, 1990

Szokolay, S.V., *Environmental Science Handbook*, Construction Press, 1980

Tabb, P., *Solar Energy Planning*, McGraw-Hill, New York, 1984

Templeton, D., *The Architecture of Sound*, Architectural Press, London, 1986

Troen, I. & Peterson, E.L., *CEC European Wind Atlas*, Riso National Laboratories, Denmark, 1989

Vale, Brenda and Robert, *Green Architecture. Design for a Sustainable Future*, Thames & Hudson, 1991

Watson, W.E., *Mechanical Services for Buildings*, Longman, London, 1992

White, Edward, *Space Adjacency Analysis*, Architectural Media, Tucson, Arizona, 1986

Williams, Graham (ed.), *Technical Handbook*, 4th edn, Thorn Lighting Ltd, Middlesex (undated)

WMO, 'Meteorological aspects of the utilisation of wind as an energy source', *Technical Note 175*, World Meteorological Organisation, Geneva, 1981

Worthington, John, 'IT: A Creative Challenge – Spinning out of Orbit', *Architects' Journal*, 2 September 1992

INDEX